WILD PEAK

Mark Hamblin

HALSGROVE
In Association with

**ENGLISH
NATURE**

First published in Great Britain in 2003

Words and photographs © copyright Mark Hamblin with the exception of:
p65 (bottom) Allan Drewitt, English Nature; p66 (all) Tony Hamblin; p71 English Nature.

British Library Cataloguing-in-Publication Data
A CIP record for this title is available from the British Library

ISBN 1 84114 288 3

Halsgrove Publishing, wishes to acknowledge
the financial support of English Nature

HALSGROVE
Halsgrove House
Lower Moor Way
Tiverton, Devon EX16 6SS
Tel: 01884 243242
Fax: 01884 243325
email: sales@halsgrove.com
website: www.halsgrove.com

Printed and bound by D'Auria Industrie Grafiche Spa, Italy

CONTENTS

Sunset over the Wheel Stones on Derwent Edge

ACKNOWLEDGEMENTS

My early interest in wildlife was ignited by a gift subscription to the Young Ornithological Club at the age of ten by Ivy and Dick Richardson, close friends of the family. This was fuelled by my father, Tony, who took me on bird-watching trips around our home in Warwickshire, rekindling his own boyhood interest in natural history. From this point onwards the seed was sown, and I wonder whether I would have taken the path into wildlife photography if it had not been for that simple birthday present and the support of my parents. Thank you!

The photographs in this book have been accumulated as a result of many hours spent out in the field but not without a great deal of assistance. A number of landowners have given me access to their land and I have also received much needed help from farmers and gamekeepers as well as from bird watchers, naturalists and bird ringers.

Wildlife photography can often be a solitary business but there are many projects that would not have been possible without the help from another like-minded photographer. For many years I have worked with Paul Hobson, an enthusiastic naturalist with a shared passion for photography, on projects such as merlin, short-eared owl, golden plover, tawny owl and badger.

Thanks must also go to Norman Lock for his help with the fox project, as well as to Simon Travis, the RSPB warden with whom I liased on the hen harriers in the Goyt Valley. There is a long list of other people who have provided me with valuable information, photographic sites and support over the years – I am most grateful to you all.

When it came to the writing of *Wild Peak*, I was initially reluctant to take on the task but was eventually persuaded by Halsgrove's Editorial Manager, Roly Smith. Thanks Roly, not only for commissioning me to write and illustrate this book, but also for your help and constructive comments during the editing stages.

I am also indebted to a number of people for their input and information on various aspects of the text, most especially Ben Le Bas at English Nature. His knowledge of insects and flowers in particular were of enormous assistance. Thanks also to Derek Crawley and Derek Yalden for their information regarding several mammal species.

Regarding the picture selection, I was pleased to be given the opportunity to decide which of my images were to be used, making the book much more of a personal representation of my photography in the Peak District. It has been a pleasure to work with the art designer Karen Binaccioni at Halsgrove, who has made an excellent job of designing the book.

Finally, I would like to say a huge thank you to Gale, my long standing partner with whom I have shared many, indeed most, of the up-and-downs of putting this book together. Gale has done all of the proof-reading as well as adding comments and making suggestions of improvements along the way and has been a source of great encouragement as well as kicking me up the backside when required! Any mistakes and omissions are all my own work.

Badger cubs in coniferous woodland

FOREWORD

By Sir Martin Doughty
Chair, English Nature

Many millions of people visit the Peak District each year, attracted by the wonderful landscape. How many go home, I wonder, with abiding memories not of the hills and dales but of the birds, animals, flowers or insects that they caught sight of?

Many thousands visit the flower-rich slopes and ash woodlands of the Derbyshire Dales National Nature Reserve. You don't have to be a botanist or even comprehend the meaning of biodiversity to be hugely impressed by the May displays of early purple orchids, cowslips and saxifrage in Cressbrook Dale.

That experience was missed in spring 2001, when the foot and mouth outbreak led to the effective closure of the country-side. When Derbyshire County Council and the Peak District National Park Authority courageously reopened the rights-of-way network on the Spring Bank Holiday weekend, thousands of frustrated walkers, kept indoors for the previous three months, flocked to the hills.

But it was not the huge turnout of hikers that made the Kinder plateau resemble Oxford Street in sales week that sticks in my memory. Rather, it was the cloudberry, that subalpine plant of wet peat bogs, flowering on the plateau like I had never seen it before, in one of its most southerly habitats. Its success that year probably resulted from the record wet autumn and winter which preceded it. Even relentless Peak District rain has a silver lining!

I'm sure that, like me, many readers will have their favourite times of the year to visit particular parts of the National Park. To watch ground-nesting birds in spring, maybe. Or flower-rich meadows in summer. Or mountain hares in winter, perhaps.

Walking northwards from my home in New Mills brings you into the National Park at Rowarth. An early April walk will find curlews flocking in the valley, the first lapwings returning to their nesting fields and, maybe, if you are lucky, snipe and short eared owl.

Mark Hamblin's excellent book provides a fascinating insight into the natural history of the Peak District. I'm sure it will give you many ideas of how you, too, can share in the enjoyment of this wonderful place.

Sir Martin Doughty

Oak leaf detail (spring)

Sphagnum mosses (summer)

Oak leaf on star moss (autumn)

Beech leaves on woodland floor (winter)

8

Chapter 1
INTRODUCTION
A Natural Heartland

Millstones under Stanage Edge

The Peak District National Park lies at the very heart of the British Isles, standing at the crossroads between the north and the south. The area was designated National Park status in 1951, the first in Britain. Then as now, it represented the last unspoilt area between the cities of Manchester and Sheffield, as well as the many other conurbations of the north Midlands.

It has always been an area for recreation providing the much needed lungs for the residents of the surrounding cities. Today, the Park attracts 22 million visits each year, making it the second most visited National Park in the world.

Few other areas in Britain can compare with the Peak District in terms of the diversity of plants, insects, birds and animals and this, combined with the rugged yet strikingly beautiful landscapes, are what endears the Park to so many people. Flower-rich grasslands which support as many as 50 plants per square metre can be found in the Derbyshire Dales, while man-made habitats – such as lead rakes and limestone quarries – support specialist flowers, orchids and breeding birds.

Traditional hay meadows, lost from much of the rest of Britain, can still be found here, allowing visitors to enjoy a colourful display of wildflowers, butterflies and farmland birds. Ancient ash woodlands cling to limestone slopes in the dales and in the north, sessile oak woodlands cloak some of the cloughs and hillsides. These habitats are exceptionally rich in wildlife and provide an important link to the past when much of the area was heavily wooded.

The wild featureless bogs formed as a result of the extensive clearances, present a contrasting picture of nodding white cotton grass and spongy sphagnum mosses. Where peat has formed over thousands of years, heather moorland prevails, which in late summer becomes a glorious sea of purple.

The Peak District landscape has been dramatically shaped by both natural and

human influences over thousands of years. Before the arrival of Stone Age people, the area was covered by dense woodlands of ash, beech, birch, elm, oak and hazel. These early settlers began to clear many of the trees to make way for grazing animals, a trend that continued over the centuries as more of the land was used for farming.

Large-scale mineral extraction and limestone quarrying have also left their mark and the damming of valleys to create reservoirs and commercial forestry have all conspired to create the rich tapestry of wildlife habitats that we enjoy today.

The varied landscape of the Park is attributable to the two principal underlying rocks, which also greatly determine the mix of habitats and associated wildlife. The central and southern regions of the Park are dominated by carboniferous limestone that was laid down 350 million years ago when the region was covered by a vast tropical sea. This area is known as the White Peak because of the light colour of the rock and is a landscape of rolling farmland criss-crossed with thousands of kilometres of drystone walls, and steep-sided dales.

The limestone plateau consists mainly of improved sheep pasture which is generally species-poor, while the remaining unimproved grasslands and hay

Gritstone rocks on Higger Tor at sunrise

Dippers are surprisingly tame along well walked routes such as Lathkill Dale

meadows support a wealth of plants, insects and other animals. The many dales which dissect the plateau have not been heavily grazed for many years because of their steep sides and consequently they support ancient ash woodlands and a profusion of wildflowers. The White Peak landscape is also heavily influenced by water that dissolves the rock, forming underground streams and caves. Where streams and rivers run on the surface, a wide variety of plant and animal life can be found in the crystal clear unpolluted waters.

Compared to the White Peak, the north and the eastern and western edges of the Park have a far more austere, rugged appearance. The principal underlying rock here is millstone grit, a sedimentary rock that was formed from sand deposits that is fused in parts with shale, formed by mud residue. These areas form the Dark Peak, named because of its sombre appearance rather than the colour of the rock.

The Dark Peak is an area of acidic heather moorland bordered by steep escarpments known as 'edges' and punctuated by dramatic rocky outcrops. The treeless dark-coloured moors are wild, desolate places which experience lower temperatures and higher precipitation compared to the limestone plateau to the south.

The heather moorlands of the Peak District represent some of the finest habitat for red grouse in the country

Consequently, the plant and animal life which is found here has to be hardy and well adapted to cope with these harsh conditions.

The contrasting habitats found within the White and Dark Peaks are the main reason why the Park supports such a wide range of wildlife species in a relatively small area. Sandwiched between the Pennines and the lowlands of the Midlands, the Peak District is also at a climatic crossroads, where both northern and southern species are able to make their homes, some at the extreme limit of their range. This adds greatly to the overall blend of wildlife that inhabits the Park, which also includes a number of rare and nationally important species.

Many areas within the Park's 1438 square kilometres (555 square miles) are specially protected or managed for wildlife in some way. Almost a third of the Park has been designated as Sites of Special Scientific Interest (SSSIs) by English Nature, the government body which is also responsible for the management of a number of Local Nature Reserves as well as the Derbyshire Dales National Nature Reserve (NNR). This flagship reserve which comprises Lathkill, Monk's, Cressbrook, Long and Hay Dales, is renowned for its sweeping limestone scenery carpeted by wild-flowers, and is one of the most visited reserves in the country.

The National Trust also manages the adjacent Biggin Dale as a NNR, making this whole area a very important site of natural heritage. Many other areas of land are owned and managed by the National Trust, whose primary objective is to safeguard these precious landscapes for the benefit of wildlife while working in conjunction with farmers and other land users to maintain a viable economical resource.

Overdale Derbyshire Wildlife Trust nature reserve comes alive with flowering heather and gorse in late summer

Other reserves are managed by the Derbyshire, Staffordshire and Yorkshire Wildlife Trusts, organisations which benefit greatly from the work of countless volunteers who carry out a range of conservation activities. Furthermore, the Peak District National Park Authority has implemented a number of conservation and management schemes so that today, some form of conservation agreement covers 80 per cent of moorland, 22 per cent of farmland and 16 per cent of woodland.

Also working within this framework are national and regional organisations such as the Royal Society for the Protection of Birds as well as local conservation and wildlife groups that form partnerships to implement key conservation projects that includes the Peak District Biodiversity Action Plan. This plan evaluates the main habitats in the Park and describes objectives for the conservation of target species within each of these habitats over a given timescale.

Much of the work of these organisations would not be possible without the help and co-operation from other landowners and farmers. There are over 2500 farms within the Peak District and these together with the nature reserves, sporting estates, reservoirs, forests and many other natural areas form a rich mosaic of habitats that is enjoyed by the millions of visitors that come to enjoy the Peak District each year.

Wild Peak, supported by English Nature, takes a seasonal look at the wildlife and natural habitats of the Peak District National Park. From the wild heather moorlands of the Dark Peak to the White Peak's flower-rich limestone dales, the book embarks on a journey around the Park's distinct habitats, through the changing seasons of the year. This is complimented by the author's 'face-to-face' accounts of photographing several charismatic species, in addition to highlighting specific conservation and environmental issues of particular significance to the Peak District.

The four seasonal chapters focus on the plants, insects, birds and mammals describing the inter-relationship between these diverse species and linking them with key habitats and specific sites. As well as serving as an insight into the lives of the region's wildlife, the book also provides inspiration and suggestions of locations to visit where the rich natural history of the Peak District can be enjoyed.

The concluding chapter takes a more pragmatic view of the current state of the Park and describes how land use as well as conservation and environmental factors may affect the region's wildlife in an uncertain future.

A rabbit stands alert on the watch for predators in a White Peak buttercup meadow

Chapter 2

SPRING

The Waking of the Year

The spring equinox, when day and night are of equal length, falls on the 21 March and marks the beginning of a season which heralds the greatest natural transformation of the Peak District landscape. The weather at this early part of the year is changeable, with cold, blustery gales and overnight frosts, followed by glorious sunny days and rising air temperatures. The weather during March sets the tempo for spring, which in recent years, following a succession of mild winters, sweeps across the region in a flush of colour.

Yellow is the prevailing colour of the early spring flowers, which vividly catch the eye and act like a magnet for emerging insects. Lesser celandines, dandelions and coltsfoot are among the first flowers to appear, and these are quickly followed by the brilliant golden flowers of marsh marigolds which light up damp meadowlands and woods. Primroses, a plant which is not overly common in the Peak, continue the yellow theme. Preferring a damp position which receives strong sunlight, primroses thrive on south-facing banks, such as those found at Froggatt close to the River Derwent.

The month of March has always been synonymous with brown hares, largely because this is the time of year when these irresistible animals can be seen engaged in their courtship antics. This behaviour involves a great deal of chasing around, leaping over one another as well as 'boxing.' Until quite recently, it was assumed that the boxing bouts were taking place between two males (bucks) fighting over the females (does). It later became apparent that these are in fact male-female confrontations where the doe boxes the ears of the amorous buck because she is not ready to mate.

The brown hare can be recognised from the rabbit by its larger body, long legs and black ear tips. They live on farmland and rough grassland as well as in woodlands. Within the Peak District their population is sparse, occurring in the fields and meadows of the White Peak as well as on the moorland edge further north. They

Dandelions en masse *in the White Peak*

Opposite: *Buttercup meadow near Winnats Pass*

15

Brown hare

are sedentary animals, feeding within a home range of around 40 hectares. They graze on a wide range of vegetation, feeding chiefly at night.

During the day, a hare will sit tight in its 'form', a small depression in the ground, where it will remain motionless with its superb camouflage. If disturbed it is capable of out-running most predators, but if it thinks it hasn't been spotted, it is possible to almost step on one before it bolts. Dawn and dusk are the best times of day to watch for hares when they are most likely to be feeding together out in the open.

Hares have a long reproductive season which begins in early January and continues until September. During this time a doe may produce three or four litters of up to four leverets. Unlike rabbits, hares spend their entire lives above ground, so the female must locate a safe place where she can give birth. Immediately after giving birth, she leaves her litter, returning for only ten minutes every 24 hours to suckle them with her rich milk.

After a few days, the leverets begin to explore their surroundings, but soon after sunset each evening they congregate back at their birthplace to await the arrival of the doe who continues to suckle them for twelve days. Strangely, when the leverets first meet up each evening there is much excitement as though they are genuinely pleased to see one another. This activity involves running in bursts of great speed. Each leveret has its own 'racetrack' where it performs extravagant acrobatic manoeuvres that may include jumping and spinning in mid-air, extended leaps and even somersaults. The reason why they perform these rituals remains a mystery.

Wheatears are most evident in flight when they flash their white rumps.

Towards the end of March, the first of the spring bird migrants have arrived back, although the exact date can vary considerable depending on weather conditions both here and along their migration route from Africa. The rather monotonous 'chiff chaff, chiff chaff' song of chiffchaffs are among the first to be heard, often from exactly the same location year after year. These small warblers only live for two or three years, but subsequent generations return to breed close to where they were reared.

Another early migrant is the wheatear, a fine upstanding bird that is widespread throughout the limestone dales and on the well-cropped grassy areas of the Dark Peak. The old name for the wheatear is 'white arse'; an apt name which perfectly describes the distinctive white rump which is evident when the bird flies. The well-marked male, complete with 'Dick Turpin' highwayman's eye stripe, can often

A female ring ouzel prepares to drop into her well-concealed nest

be spotted perched proudly on a prominent stone as he delivers his short warbling song in early spring. The female chooses the nest site, which is often situated under a boulder or within a drystone wall, where the chicks are better protected from predators.

Under the gritstone edges of the Dark Peak, newly-arrived male ring ouzels proclaim their territory with a succession of five clear notes while perched on a solitary rowan or birch. The ring ouzel, is a member of the thrush family, sometimes referred to as a 'mountain blackbird', although one writer once described it as 'a blackbird in a dinner jacket', which aptly describes the male's dusky appearance and while bib.

Ring ouzels generally nest above the tree line on a rock ledge, but they will also nest in deep heather and even in old farm buildings. During the breeding season they often become very secretive, making them difficult to observe. However, when they have young chicks to feed, the male can sometimes be seen foraging for worms in the sheep-grazed upland fields. The first brood have usually left the nest by mid-May but a pair will often raise a second and occasionally third brood prolonging the nesting season well into July.

Upland grazing pastures are favoured feeding areas for ring ouzels and wheatears

Whinchats are one of the last species to return to the moors, chiefly because their favoured food of caterpillars and other grubs are not in abundance until late spring. Upland areas which offer good cover of heather or bracken, such as below Stanage Edge, are ideal habitats for whinchats to breed. The best way to locate the male is to listen out for his attractive warbler-like song which he delivers from a prominent perch during May. Seen close-up, he is a handsome bird with an orange chest and black and white head, often bobbing his tail in a restless manner.

Above left: Large stands of bracken provide whinchats with a secure place to nest

Above right: Cuckoos can be heard calling from late April onwards

One of the most familiar sounds of the spring is the call of the cuckoo; a bird best known for its parasitic, egg laying behaviour. The image of a tiny wren or dunnock feeding a greedy young cuckoo while standing on its back is one of the strangest sights in nature. The adopted parents of this huge 'monster' with its insatiable appetite have to work flat out in an attempt to silence the youngster's calls for food.

The cuckoo is able to mimic the eggs of many species, but each individual female usually has a favourite host. She is able to reproduce the markings of her chosen host's eggs with remarkable accuracy, a skill that is passed on to her female offspring. Moorland with scattered trees or birch scrubland is the best habitat in which to find cuckoos where they most often lay their eggs in the nest of meadow pipits, a bird that is very common in the uplands. Although the cuckoo's call is unmistakable, its long wings and tail give it the appearance of a sparrowhawk or kestrel when seen in flight.

During early April the moors come alive with the calls of the many wading birds which return each spring to breed. Upland areas such as the Howden and Langsett Moors and Bleaklow are recognised as among some of Britain's most important breeding grounds for golden plover, snipe and curlew. The bubbling calls of a curlew as it rises steeply into the sky before gliding gracefully back down to earth is

Face-to-face with... Red Foxes

Sitting silently in the confines of my hide in the twilight of dawn, I was willing the cubs to appear from their earth only 20 metres away. Soon the sun crept over the horizon and, right on cue, the inquisitive face of one of the cubs appeared at the main entrance.

The cub's gaze was fixed towards the bottom of the field where I could just make out the vixen trotting purposefully towards the earth. She quickly made her way along a well-worn path but before she could reach the earth the cubs burst into life and ran excitedly to meet her. As one, they dived underneath their mother and began to suckle although it was clear that the vixen was less than keen on the attention of five sets of razor-sharp teeth.

The female suckled her cubs for less than a minute and then, after regurgitating some food for her youngsters, quickly stole away through the hedgerow. With food in their bellies, the cubs had plenty of energy and they soon began to play in the early morning sunshine. This involved chasing, gambolling and leaping into the air performing mock pounces. At times, one or two of the cubs came within a few metres of the hide, although they never seemed to be aware of my presence. After ten minutes of this excited activity, the cubs disappeared back underground leaving me to reflect on what had just unfolded before me.

I have always had a great fascination for foxes, but despite numerous attempts. this was the first time that I had secured any decent pictures. Nevertheless, this project was not without its disappointments and I experienced many fruitless mornings in the hide without success. If the weather was poor I often didn't enter the hide at all but instead watched from my car on the edge of the field. I soon learnt that the vixen made regular visits to her cubs, arriving at almost the same time each morning. One of these visits was just before sunrise, which meant I had to be in the hide by 4 am to avoid being spotted.

Generally this worked well, but on one occasion I was within 10 metres of the hide when I heard a loud bark. I looked up to see the vixen, fully aware of my presence, barking an alarm to her cubs. Unsure what to do, I pretended that I hadn't seen her and casually walked well away. I waited a minute or so and then slowly peered from my hiding place. The vixen was still looking towards the earth, but realising that the danger had passed, she continued on her way across the fields.

On my return a few days later I was in the hide well before dawn but saw no sign of activity until 6.30 am when one of the larger cubs emerged from the earth. A second cub soon joined its sibling to sit quietly in the warm sunshine. After a while the cubs started to pick over the remains of a rabbit but from their satiated appearance, they had apparently fed well.

Now that the cubs were well grown I knew that my project was drawing to a close. Soon they would have to fend for themselves but for a while longer they still had the willing vixen to provide for them and they could bask in the warmth of another fine spring morning.

A vixen suckles her cubs in the early morning sunshine

surely one of the finest sounds of spring. Its aerial display is repeated with long drawn out 'cour-lie, cour-lie' calls which build slowly in an excited crescendo, as the bird hangs buoyantly in the air.

The damp bogs of the Dark Peak also resonate to the sounds of 'drumming' snipe. This extraordinary noise is made when air rushes through the snipe's wing primaries and outer tail feathers as it drops in a rapid descent from high in flight. This impressive display forms part of the bird's courtship, and is most frequently heard on still mornings in early spring. They are not easy to spot in the air and even more difficult while on the ground; their cryptic plumage blending perfectly with the surrounding reeds and sedges.

Lapwings are traditionally birds of lowland pasture, but they also breed in low numbers in some upland areas. On the moorlands they seem to favour areas of burnt heather where they can nest on open ground which affords them good all-round vision to spot potential danger. Like many waders, their courtship displays are performed in the air. The pair perform tumbling acrobatics accompanied by throbbing wing beats and distinctive 'pee-wit' calls. As they twist and turn with incredible agility, the sun picks out the metallic green of their plumage which gives rise to their alternative name of green plover.

By contrast, the golden plover is far more elusive, although its melancholy calls can be heard floating on the breeze throughout the spring. This so-called 'guardian of the moors' has an almost ventriloquial call which varies in volume as it moves its head from side to side, making it very difficult to pinpoint its exact position. The 'golden' name refers to the brilliant golden-brown upper parts which sparkle in the sunlight. Front-on, the bird appears much darker, the black belly extending well up the chest and throat in some individuals.

Above left: The curlew's streaky brown plumage provides camouflage at the nest

Above right: The tumbling display flights of lapwings are a welcome sight in April

Opposite page: The rocky outcrop of Over Owler Tor forms part of Hathersage Moor

23

The Peak District uplands support nationally important breeding populations of golden plover

Outside the breeding season, golden plovers lose their black underparts and form large flocks often associating with lapwings. In winter these flocks can be found feeding on arable farmland and rough grassland well away from their breeding grounds. However, as spring approaches, small parties of golden plover may be seen at lower elevations, perhaps feeding in sheep pastures, where they engage in courtship displays. Once the worst of the winter weather has subsided the birds return to their traditional moorland sites where they continue their courtship and establish territories.

On some of the high plateaux they breed in high densities and are sometimes joined by the diminutive dunlin. These two moorland specialities are often found in similar habitat lending significance to the dunlin's long-standing nickname of 'plover's page'. Within the Peak, the dunlin has always been a rare breeding bird, preferring instead the highlands and islands of Scotland further north. When heard, its trilling call often takes you by surprise, but it is a most welcome sound which is a fitting accompaniment to the haunting piping of its master.

With over three quarters of the National Park used for farming in some way, this industry is a key part of the economy for local people, and it is also an important habitat for wildlife. There are close to 2500 farms in the Peak District, although most of these are small – less than 40 hectares (100 acres). Just over half of the Park is enclosed farmland, while much of the rest of the land provides rough grazing for sheep, particularly on the moorlands of the Dark Peak.

A classic view of White Peak farmland from Bretton Edge

The vast majority of the enclosed farmland is found on the White Peak plateau, a landscape characterised by its patchwork of green fields and drystone walls. Much of this limestone plateau is 'improved' rye-grass leys or pasture which is regularly ploughed, re-seeded and fertilised to maximise productivity. These bright green monocultures are of low wildlife value when compared with the species-rich traditional hay meadows which once prevailed over much of this landscape. Sadly, they are now reduced to only a few specially-protected sites.

The national declines in farmland birds are mirrored within the Peak District, with many bird populations down by over 50 per cent. Nevertheless there are small pockets of land where birds are able to thrive. Ancient hedgerows and rough field margins and are of particular importance for birds such as linnet, bullfinch, yellowhammer, whitethroat, song thrush and grey partridge. Each of these species has its own specific requirements, but the key to all their survival is an abundance of insects during the breeding season.

Other farmland birds such as skylark and lapwing favour more open habitats in which to breed. The never-ending liquid song of skylarks singing high overhead is one of the most familiar of all the springtime sounds. They often remain in the same position for long periods, sometimes beyond the sight of the naked eye. They build their nests directly on the ground, perhaps in an old hoof mark or in a tussock of vegetation. The chicks develop very quickly and leave the nest after only eight or nine days, although they are still unable to fly. By dispersing in different directions, the chicks have a better individual chance of escaping predation, a strategy adopted by a number of ground-nesting birds.

The farmed plateau of the White Peak is intersected by a number of limestone dales, five of which form the Derbyshire Dales National Nature Reserve. The reserve's dales – Lathkill, Cressbrook, Monk's, Long and Hay – represent superb examples of all of the major habitats of the White Peak Natural Area. By late April, cowslips cover many of the dalesides and begin a succession of flowers that will continue throughout the spring and summer. Throughout Cressbrook Dale, a mass of early purple orchids decorate the steep banks in a wash of colour which is a perfect foil to the rocky outcrop known as Peter's Stone.

In common with most of the country, the Peak District was once almost exclusively wooded before the woods were felled and cleared by early settlers. Today, the landscape is very different from that inherited by Stone Age people, but classic examples

Above: The attractive song of the song thrush includes a broad repertoire of often-repeated phrases

Below: The liquid song of skylarks fills the air high above the White Peak

of ancient woodlands can still be found. Most notably these are the sessile oakwoods of the Derbyshire Wildlife Trust's reserve at Ladybower Wood and the National Trust's Padley Gorge, near Grindleford. Both are exceptionally rich in wildlife and this is especially evident during May when the woods reverberate with bird song.

A woodland dawn chorus is something that everyone should try to experience at least once, and there is no better place than Padley Gorge at 5 am on a sunny May morning. It doesn't really matter if you don't know a wood warbler from a wood-pecker; the sheer joy of listening to the cacophony of sounds emanating from the trees makes the early wake-up well worth the effort.

The Peak's sessile oakwoods are home to a range of bird species such as robin, song thrush and members of the tit family which return to the woods to breed, perhaps having spent the winter in nearby gardens. Other species such as nuthatch,

Opposite page: Early purple orchids in Cressbrook Dale

Sessile oak woodland on the Ladybower Wood DWT reserve

Face-to-face with... Short-eared Owls

As the sun dropped towards the horizon, warming the landscape with a golden light, a short-eared owl began to stir from its daytime roost. After a quick ruffle of its feathers it launched into the air and with gentle wing beats made its way effortlessly towards one of its favoured hunting areas. As it quartered the ground in search of field voles the late sun shone though its giant moth-like wings, giving it an almost otherworldly appearance.

Even with the naked eye, the pale-coloured owl stood out clearly against the dark moorland. At first gliding but then, having detected a potential meal, it stalled, hovering perfectly just above its intended victim. After pin-pointing the noise the owl dropped like a stone, talons out-stretched into the long grass. After a brief pause it took to the air clutching a small rodent and headed purposefully in the direction of its secluded nest site.

Earlier in March, I had watched the male court the female with his dramatic aerial display. Climbing high into the air he glided briefly, before tumbling earthwards, clapping his wings together and delivering a booming 'hoo hoo hoo' call. Impressed by his antics, the female flew to join him and the bond was sealed. Shortly afterwards the female selected a nest site in deep heather, well protected from the elements and concealed from predators.

She laid her seven eggs over a period of around 12-14 days but unlike most birds (which only begin to incubate at the end of egg laying), owls begin incubating after they have laid the first egg. Consequently, the chicks hatch at daily or two day intervals so that by the time the last egg has hatched the first chick may be two weeks old. There is good reason for this nesting strategy, for in years when food is scarce, the youngest chicks may starve or be killed thereby providing food for the eldest siblings. Although this cannibalism may seem barbaric to us, it is a very effective survival mechanism.

After three weeks incubation, the first chick emerged from its shell, followed over subsequent days by its six siblings so that eventually the nest resembled a set of Russian dolls. With hungry chicks to feed the male stepped up his hunting and I watched him on many afternoons patrolling the grasslands as early as 4pm. In good vole years he can find prey relatively easily and may even cache prey at a separate site. However, in leaner times or as a result of bad weather which blighted this pair, it is not unusual for only one or two chicks to fledge successfully.

Well before they could fly, the three surviving chicks left the nest and dispersed amongst the heather, travelling over 100m from their birthplace thus giving them a better chance of remaining undetected from predators. With both parents now hunting for prey the chicks grew quickly and they were soon on the wing, although it would be some time before they are able to emulate the methodical hunting skills of their parents.

Short-eared owls often use posts for hunting

treecreeper and woodpeckers tend to remain in the woodlands throughout the year, tapping and probing at decaying trees for signs of insect life hidden deep inside the rotting wood. Towards the end of April, summer migrants such as pied and spotted flycatcher, redstart, tree pipit and wood warbler join the massing throngs to feed on the hordes of insects found in the canopy.

Once the leaves appear on the trees casting concealing shadows, woodland birds can be infuriatingly difficult to locate by sight. Indeed, this is the main reason why many species have such loud songs. Basically, they are all communicating a similar message; 'Here I am and this is my patch.' To a female, this may entice her to investigate the resident male's territory, whereas to a male it triggers a response of either fight or flee.

Although here in the Peak District we are not serenaded by the finest of the woodland choristers, the nightingale, there are some admirable stand-ins. Both song thrushes and blackbirds have attractive liquid songs which they deliver from high in the canopy. Blackcaps and garden warblers are also delightful songsters, their melodious phrases belying their somewhat plain appearance. The wood warbler is a speciality of these sessile oakwoods. It is best recognised by its song which begins gently with a repeated 'sip sip sip' and accelerates towards a finale which culminates in a rapid trill.

Perhaps the most amazing song of all is that of the diminutive wren. This tiny bird explodes into song from low bushes and brambles throughout the woodland and provides the background noise throughout the woods at most times of the day. Robins too, sing their wistful song from a favoured perch throughout the day, and interestingly, this is one of few species where both male and female join in the chorus together.

In addition to the sweet warbles of the songbirds, there are other species that participate in the dawn chorus, although they are perhaps not as well equipped as others in terms of harmony. Nuthatches make an excited and musical 'tueeh' which signals their position high up in the branches. Once the male has attracted a mate, the pair will busy themselves searching for a suitable nest site, often an old woodpecker hole. To escape predation, the pair collects mud which they daub around the entrance to their adopted home to reduce the diameter of the hole.

Green woodpeckers are among the most vociferous throughout the spring, especially during courtship. Their call is a far-reaching 'yaffle' or laughing cry that is repeated many times as the pair communicate to each other. These exchanges may be followed by a game of tag on their nesting tree, as the pair chase each other around the trunk. Padley Woods is one of their favoured breeding habitats although you are most likely to see them foraging on the anthills which dot the grounds of the nearby Longshaw Lodge.

The redstart, so named because of its bright red-orange tail, is one of the most attractive woodland inhabitants. The colourful males return to their familiar haunts a few days before the females in order to establish a territory through long bouts of robin-like warbling song. As part of the courtship, the male chases the female from branch to branch, both birds constantly quivering and flicking their tails in a dramatic fashion. Like many woodland species, redstarts choose to nest in holes and may take up residence in a decaying tree or drystone wall, although they will also use a nest box.

Pied flycatchers have also benefited from nest box schemes. This has been very evident in Ladybower and Padley Woods as well as the Derbyshire

Above: *The raucous calls of green woodpecker can be heard throughout Padley Gorge*

Left: *Redstarts frequent sessile oakwoods as well as many of the dales in the White Peak*

Above left: *A male pied flycatcher in Ladybower Wood where they make good use of nest boxes*

Above right: *A female woodcock incubates her eggs*

Wildlife Trust's Hillbridge Woods reserve, where the population of these charming black and white birds has risen significantly. Inevitably there is stiff competition for nest sites, not only among the flycatchers but also from the resident blue and great tits which have been house-hunting since early April. Unwavering in their quest to secure a nest site, the male flycatchers sing enthusiastically and flit from box to box in search of a vacant dwelling place.

By the time that the female flycatchers arrive, most males will have established a territory and will be defending several possible nest sites from which the female can make her choice. During this period, the male sings his jolly jingle and flicks his wings excitedly as he escorts his mate on an inspection of the nest boxes. With luck the female will find a box to her liking and the pair will then begin nest building.

Unlike the majority of the woodland dwellers, the woodcock prefers to keep a low profile most of the time. It is one of the few birds that relies exclusively on camouflage to remain undetected while silently incubating its eggs. The plumage of this woodland wader is a beautiful mix of browns that make it almost impossible to spot when it is sat motionless on its nest among the old autumn leaves. But as dusk descends, the male reveals himself by flying repeatedly over his breeding woodland, emitting a soft croaking call. This 'roding' display flight is best seen during May, when the male's stocky silhouette can be seen flying just above the trees.

As night descends, tawny owls begin to call to each other before setting off on a night's hunting. They hunt primarily for wood mice and other small mammals but will also take birds, frogs and earthworms. Within the woodland, they often sit

A tawny owl on the look-out for an easy meal

The Great Divide

The geographical position of the Peak District at the crossroads of highland and lowland Britain makes it an interesting area for species at the extremes of their natural range.

Two plants at their northerly limit are dark mullein and stemless thistle. Dark mullein is a tall plant with yellow flowers which favours well-drained calcareous (limestone) soil and is found at two or three sites including Bradford Dale.

Stemless thistle is common in southern England but reaches no further north than the Peak District. This small plant grows as a flat rosette with a single purple flower head at its centre. It is widely known as the 'picnic thistle' because of its liking for growing on closely-grazed calcareous grassland where it gives no warning of the sharp spines lurking among the inviting green turf.

There are also a good number of plants in the Peak on the southern edge of their range, several of which also favour the limestone soils of the White Peak. Melancholy thistle is a handsome plant with large purple flowers on a spineless stem, features which are in sharp contrast to its irritating southern relative. It is a perennial herb of upland hay meadows, damp grassland and open woods and fine examples can be found in Monk's Dale.

Jacob's ladder is among the finest of Peak District flowers and is a true northern specialist, occurring only here and in the Yorkshire Dales and Northumberland. The name 'Jacob's-ladder' refers to the story in Genesis and derives from the pinnate, ladder-like leaves that reach up to the heavens. Its beautiful spires of bright blue flowers decorate the slopes of Lathkill Dale and the Dove Valley during June and July.

High on the tops of the Kinder Plateau, cloudberry forms large mats of vegetation. This classic subalpine species is confined to the wet peat bogs of the Peak District northwards, but at these lower altitudes it rarely fruits unlike in Norway where the orange berries are highly sought after. Of all the plants on the limits of their distribution none are more tenuous than the glacial relic, alpine cinquefoil. During the last Ice Age, many plant species spread south but as the ice retreated most moved back northwards, dying out in southern Britain. However some, like alpine cinquefoil, held on and today a single plant maintains a toe-hold in the Peak District.

In the bird world, one species on the northern limit of its range is the hobby, a rare breeding raptor found in the south of the Peak District. These dashing falcons prey on swallows as well as dragonflies, which they spectacularly eat on the wing. As a breeding species, the golden plover and twite are at the southern end of their range in England here, although golden plover also breed in Wales. Occasionally, fieldfares have also nested in the Peak District, a species more at home much further north in Scandinavia.

One mammal that has made its home here and represents the only population south of Scotland is the mountain or blue hare. This species was introduced into the Peak in Victorian times and has subsequently prospered. Mountain hares are now a common sight in the Dark Peak, and are especially noticeable because of their habit of changing the colour of their coat to white in winter. There are thriving populations on the Kinder Plateau and the Derwent Moors. Their presence is a welcome addition to the rich wildlife of the Peak District and provides a further link to our northern relatives.

Jacob's ladder growing in its Peak District stronghold in Lathkill Dale

Wood mice are common in woodlands and form the staple diet for tawny owls

motionless on a favoured branch overlooking a clearing, listening intently for any noise. The sounds of wood mice scuttling around among the leaf litter are easily detected on a still night and once their position is pinpointed, the owl swoops down on broad, silent wings to snatch its prey.

Nightfall is also the signal for some of the other woodland characters to emerge form their daytime slumber. Badger cubs which were born in late winter now appear above ground for the first time and, with patience, they can be watched close to their underground homes. The sow gives birth to up to four cubs in February but they remain in their underground labyrinth for around two months. They grow quickly on their mother's rich supply of milk so that by the time they raise their heads above the parapet in late April they are almost two thirds fully-grown.

Above ground they remain near the sett entrance, taking in the smells and sounds of the woodland. The sow stays close-by and spends her time grooming them, searching for ticks and other skin parasites, while the cubs join in with bouts of vigorous scratching. The cubs keep themselves occupied by playing boisterously with their mother, pushing and nuzzling against her larger frame as they test their strength and develop their skills. Despite her playful nature, the sow remains vigilant and at the slightest unfamiliar noise or smell she signals the cubs to bolt back to the sanctuary of the sett.

For a few brief weeks during spring this frenetic activity is paralleled by an explosion of plant growth as the countryside takes on a different persona by the day.

Badger cubs feeding near their sett at dusk

Opposite page: A carpet of bluebells benefits from the open springtime canopy

There are certainly many natural harbingers of spring – the first swallow or the first song of the cuckoo – but there are none more visually appealing than a dazzling display of brightly-coloured bluebells shimmering on a woodland floor. The bluebell is one of Britain's most charismatic and best loved plants, for there is nowhere else in the world that this charming flower can be found growing in such profusion.

As well as their wonderful display of colour, there is a lot more to this habitat than meets the eye. A rich variety of wildlife flourishes within these open woodlands, much of which is a lot easier to see before the canopy of leaves shuts out the sunshine. For the bluebells themselves it is always a race against time, for they must grow, flower and set seed before the canopy casts its shade over the woodland floor.

Although the name 'bluebell' is now widely accepted, the plant has been attributed a number of names over the years. It is also known as 'culverkeys', 'auld mans bells', 'ring o' bells' and 'jacinth', while in Scotland it is still referred to as 'wild hyacinth'. Some may say that even the name 'bluebell' is misleading, as the flowers only appear blue in overcast conditions. On sunny days, they look purple, as anyone who has tried to photograph them in bright sunshine will testify.

In early spring, the open woodland floor is covered with other flowers including lesser celandine, wood anemone and primrose. Dotted between the bluebells, there is an understorey dominated by young trees of birch, hazel and field maple and shrubs of holly, hawthorn and dogwood. Overhead, the mature trees of oak, beech and ash form a canopy layer, but as yet their leaves remain in tight buds.

The Peak's woodlands also provide habitat for hundreds of insect species which are so important as a food source for other wildlife, including the curiously-named hairy-eyed wood ant. These co-operative insects are major scavengers and predators of other invertebrates in their favoured habitat of sessile oak woodland. Their prominent nest mounds which they build in exposed sunny sites along woodland rides and in clearings are very noticeable throughout Padley Woods. In suitable habitat such as this, they can sustain numerous colonies which may be linked by trails to form supercolonies.

High above in the canopy, literally thousands of caterpillars and other insects are munching their way through the emerging green foliage. By timing their breeding season to coincide with this plentiful larder of protein-rich goodies, many birds are often able to successfully raise large broods. Some, like the blue tit, may have as many as 15 hungry mouths to feed. One recent sixteen-hour vigil of a nest box containing eight chicks revealed that the adults made 635 visits, each chick receiving 79 juicy morsels – assuming their parents were feeding democratically.

These high rates of productivity among many common species have direct implications for the success of several predators. The sparrowhawk, like many of the region's raptors, was a rare sight in the Peak District forty years ago as a consequence of the widespread use of deadly organochlorine pesticides. These poisons accumulated in the bodies of songbirds on which sparrowhawks often preyed, and the population consequently crashed. Here in the Peak District they have recovered well, breeding throughout the region and spreading into both urban and suburban areas.

Today, these handsome hawks can regularly be seen hunting through woodlands, and along hedgerows as well as venturing into gardens to grab unwary victims from bird tables. Some people may argue that there are now too many and that the high numbers of sparrowhawks is having a detrimental effect on songbird populations. However, research has shown that this is not the case and in fact breeding bird populations in woodlands have remained constant even though sparrowhawk numbers have increased.

Sparrowhawks, like all predators, generally prey upon 'surplus' birds that would otherwise die of ill health, starvation or hard weather. Young blue tits and other fledglings quickly have to become street-wise if they are to stay alive long enough to breed the following year. This natural selection ensures that the weak and sick are weeded out while the fittest, fastest and strongest birds will survive to breed and raise healthy offspring.

Spring appears to arrive very late to the ancient ashwoods which cling to the steep dalesides of the White Peak. While all around other trees and plants are pushing forth fresh green leaves, the ash remains bare, its characteristic black tipped branches keeping the new foliage tightly under wraps. This late emergence of leaves is the key reason why ashwoods are such an important habitat for many flowers. Maximum daylight is able to penetrate beneath the skimpily clad limbs, allowing a profusion of wildflowers to flourish well into summer.

The ashwoods of the White Peak are the largest and most important examples of this habitat in Britain. Following the Parliamentary Enclosure Movement and the improvement of the limestone plateau in the eighteenth and early nineteenth

This colourful male sparrowhawk takes a rest from hunting

Protecting the Birds

The Peak Birds Project launched in 2001 is a joint venture funded by the Peak District National Park Authority and the RSPB. It works closely with English Nature and the Department for the Environment, Food and Rural Affairs in an attempt to safeguard upland birds.

Three species – curlew, lapwing and twite – were identified in the Peak District Biodiversity Action Plan (BAP) as needing special help. The key to the success of the project is habitat conservation through partnerships with farmers and landowners, and this has been the main work of the Project Officer, Chris Tomson.

During the first year, 140 farmers were contacted with many entering into management agreements. Minor management changes can have a major impact on bird populations while some habitats simply need securing to protect existing breeding birds.

Three important habitats have been targeted by the project for special attention. Flower rich hay meadows are a scarce but valuable commodity providing vital food for twite. Second broods of twite are fed primarily on the seeds of sorrel, a common plant of meadows that flowers in late June and July. So conservation of hay meadows which are cut after this date is an effective but simple way of helping this threatened species.

Wet pasture is the most important habitat for breeding waders in the Peak District. Curlew, lapwing and snipe can all be found on in-bye land – where moorland meets farmland pasture – but this is often the least attractive land to farmers. However, farmers can enter agri-environment schemes that provides them with the financial help needed to protect these key areas. On arable farmland the recently-introduced Arable Stewardship Scheme rewards farmers for growing spring cereals and leaving stubbles over winter, a measure that will greatly benefit breeding lapwings. Corners of fields will also be planted to provide wild bird seed for farmland birds such as yellowhammers, linnets and greenfinches.

Overall, farmers and landowners have been overwhelmingly supportive of the Peak Birds Project and many are keen to help farmland birds but simply need advice on what best to do. One farmer described how: "I had always marked nests before ploughing, harrowing or rolling my grassland in the spring, but there just isn't the staff on farms to do it now". Happily the project officer is arranging for someone to mark nests for this farmer in the future.

The ultimate aim of the project is to increase populations of these key bird species by securing and effectively managing suitable habitats, in adddition to boosting farm incomes through agri-environment schemes. By the end of its first year, the project had helped farmers apply for more than £200,000 through DEFRA's Environmentally Sensitive Area and Countryside Stewardship Schemes. These ten-year agreements will support conservation measures for birds and bring crucial reward payments to supplement farmers' incomes.

Lapwing numbers have increased on many upland farms through projects such as Operation Lapwing and the Peak Birds Project

Above left: *Ancient ashwoods cloak the steep dalesides of Lathkill Dale*

Above right: *Slow worms are difficult to spot, preferring to spend their time under rocks and in dense vegetation*

Spring sandwort, known locally as lead-wort, growing on a lead spoil heap

centuries, grazing pressure on the dales relaxed, leading to an expansion of semi-natural ash woodland. This together with the re-colonisation of quarries and mining areas has led to a marked increase in ash woodland over the last two hundred years. Particularly fine examples include Dovedale, Cressbrook Dale, Lathkill Dale and the Via Gellia.

These ashwoods are among the richest habitats for wildlife found in the uplands. Dominated by ash, they also share the canopy with oaks and both small and large-leaved limes. Many ashwoods also contained wych elms as a common species, although this has largely disappeared as a result of the ravages of Dutch elm disease. Despite this, it remains as an important shrub layer species where coppiced and is the food plant for the white-letter hairstreak butterfly, which is now in danger in both Britain and Europe. The many skeletons of mature elm trees also provide vital deadwood habitat for many rare beetles, flies and other invertebrates.

Wood anemone, ramsons, bluebells and yellow archangel carpet the lower slopes, with the more unusual columbine and lily-of-the-valley favouring the higher stony dalesides. Other specialities include mezereon, once known as 'paradise plant' due to the heady fragrance of its February flowers. Unfortunately many specimens were dug up and transplanted into cottage gardens and now it occurs very rarely in these calcareous woods. Slow worms and noctule and pipistrelle bats are also typical here, and the woodland is a valuable habitat for many snails which require a high calcium intake.

The White Peak ashwoods often link to other important habitats which include grasslands, heath, rock faces, scree and lead rakes. This latter man-made habitat is

the surface spoil heaps of waste material from centuries of lead mining. Most plants and flowers are unable to tolerate the toxic nature of these spoil heaps, but there are a few specialised exceptions which are able to flourish. One is spring sandwort, known locally as leadwort, which forms dense carpets of small white flowers over the old workings in places like Magpie Mine, near Sheldon.

Also growing in these grasslands, but difficult to spot, is moonwort, a relative of the fern family. This tiny plant of no more than 5-6cm in height, has a single fleshy leaf surrounding a spike which sheds the spores. Also found on lead spoil heaps are alpine scurvygrass and alpine penny-cress. The latter is a tall fleshy-leaved plant topped with small bunches of white or purple flowers and is a 'hyper-accumulator' of a range of metals including lead. Elsewhere, this has led to some interesting experiments, using it as a natural cleanser of toxic waste sites. The cresses are planted on the contaminated soil where they are left to take up the metals and then simply pulled up and removed.

Mountain pansies grace the spring grasslands on the Priestcliffe Lees DWT reserve

During May and into June, the hummocks that characterise the spoil heaps come alive with hundreds of nodding, bright yellow mountain pansies. Although not a lead grassland specialist it is often found alongside other common species such as bird's-foot trefoil, eyebright and sorrel which are also remarkably lead-tolerant. Around some of the old spoil heaps above Via Gellia, herb Paris can also be found growing. This woodland species is regarded as an indicator of ancient woodland; its presence here, along with bluebells, suggesting that this area was cleared-felled for mining operations, but has never been cultivated or farmed.

The pace of spring is unrelenting as the days become increasingly longer and the countryside greens with new growth. Even before the season is out, many birds have fledged their young. The chicks of blackbirds and thrushes beg their parents for food on town park lawns. Mallards, coots and moorhens all have chicks on the water and young ravens squawk high on the cliffs of Kinder. The abundance of insects makes feeding a breeze for swallows and house martins as they hawk over the meadows, where the long grass also provides good cover for foxes to snatch unsuspecting young rabbits. As spring drifts slowly into summer, life is becoming much easier for many of the Peak's inhabitants.

The diminutive moonwort

View across Edale towards Lose Hill in high summer

Chapter 3
SUMMER
When the Living is Easy

As summer advances, the masses of early purple orchids which decorated Cressbrook Dale during May still remain, but the deep purple flower spikes are dying back, their job of attracting insects complete for another year. The woodlands flowers are also fading away under the darkening canopy. Now it is the turn of another myriad of floral displays to come to the fore in the hay meadows, dalesides and along roadside verges.

Old Dale, to the west of Chee Dale, forms part of the Derbyshire Wildlife Trust nature reserve and is a fine example of a wildflower field. During spring, plants such as cowslip and salad burnet can be found here and these are later followed by

Field scabious attracts many butterflies, bees and other insects

up to six species of orchids. In July look for the lilac flowers of field scabious also known by the vernacular names of pincushion flower, lady's pincushion and blue bonnet's. The term 'scabious' is derived form the Latin name: Scabiosa herba – the herb used to treat scabies.

Chee Dale itself is well known for its spectacular limestone cliffs which dominate the western end of the dale, and these provide suitable nest sites for a small colony of house martins. The cliffs are also notable for rock whitebeam, an uncommon tree with distinctive white undersides to its leaves which are clearly visible as they flutter in the breeze. Along the cliff tops, the purple flowers of common knapweed attract peacock, red admiral and small tortoiseshell butterflies as well as several species of bee.

Elsewhere in the dale there are colonies of Jacob's ladder, a nationally rare plant. The true native distribution for this handsome species with its spires of bright blue flowers is confined to grassland and scree slopes in the Peak District. Along the south-facing slopes of the dale, bloody crane's-bill, hawkbit and common rock rose make a colourful display of purple and yellow, the latter serving as the food plant for the day-flying cistus forester moth. This small metallic green moth can be seen shimmering over south-facing unimproved grassland throughout June.

Above: *The limestone cliffs of Chee Dale support a range of wildlife*

Right: *Bloody crane's-bill and hawkbit flowering on the south-facing slopes of Chee Dale*

Far left: *Musk thistle*

Left: *Bee orchids can be common one year but scarce the next*

High above the River Wye, Chee Tor is covered by a mixture of harebells, butter-cups and musk thistle, a species recognised by its 'nodding' purple flower heads. Continuing into Miller's Dale, common spotted orchids and a host of other flowers adorn the footpath. Once again the Derbyshire Wildlife Trust has a presence here, managing the disused quarries as nature reserves. You can enter the reserve close to the old lime kilns a few hundred metres east of Miller's Dale station. The lime kilns were once used to burn the limestone to form quicklime for the chemical and steel industries and was also used by hill farmers to neutralise acidic moorland to help create grazing pasture.

Today the quarry provides the ideal habitat for several species of orchid, including the diminutive bee and frog orchids, twayblade and a thriving colony of fragrant orchids. If you visit on a hot day in July when the fragrant orchids are in full bloom, the air is filled with their clove-like scent.

Most orchids are easily recognised by their very intricate flowers on tall spikes. A whole range of pollinators that includes bees, wasps, flies and moths are attracted to the brightly marked flowers. Some, like the bee orchid have flowers that are cunningly designed to act as mimics. A male bee, on seeing what it believes to be an attractive female, lands on the lip of the bee orchid's flower and attempts to mate. In the process, a small sticky package of pollen is dabbed onto its back, which hitches a lift to the next bee orchid where it leads to cross-pollination.

47

Face-to-face with... Badgers

As dusk closed in, a robin sang its last ditty of the day while all around blackbirds chattered their incessant alarm calls. After a while the woodland fell quiet, but the silence was soon shattered as a wood pigeon alighted in the tree above me. Every sound seemed to be exaggerated in the still night air, so much so that I hardly dare breathe for fear of betraying my presence. As the gloom enveloped the woodland I kept my eyes locked on the hole 10 metres away – waiting and hoping.

After what seemed like an eternity but was perhaps no more than half an hour, I glimpsed a movement at the entrance hole. A few seconds later the unmistakable black and white head of a badger came into view. Even at this late hour, the white stripes appeared bright and I could clearly see the animal sniffing the air for any signs of danger before fully emerging above ground.

Badgers have an acute sense of smell, which serves as their primary means of identifying danger as well as for food and other badgers. They also react keenly to noises and tend to be more wary on windy nights as both of their principal senses are severely impaired. However, on this still evening, the badger had little to fear and soon began to relax.

Having plonked itself down on its hindquarters, it proceeded to scratch and groom its coat. With no other sounds to interfere, I could clearly hear the badger's claw running through its wiry coat. In fact, I became so absorbed that I hadn't noticed that a second individual had emerged from a nearby hole. The two animals greeted each other briefly, the second remaining in the entrance of the sett where it too engaged in grooming.

The first badger had now finished its ablutions and promptly disappeared down another hole but soon reappeared pausing momentarily before heading off into the darkness. I waited a few more minutes but I was now struggling to see anything and so reluctantly, I quietly retraced my steps through the woodland.

From the amount of used bedding that I had previously seen outside the holes, I was convinced that there were cubs in residence. They would surely soon be emerging for their first look at the outside world and so I vowed to return in a few days' time.

My second visit confirmed my suspicions as I watched two cubs boldly follow the sow as she emerged into the woodland. A few nights later four fluffy cubs accompanied their mother from the sett, and I subsequently spent six months watching and photographing these siblings as they grew into adult badgers. Some of my most memorable encounters took place during July by which time the cubs had become independent of their mother and were active in broad daylight.

Having this opportunity to watch badgers at close quarters and knowing that I had their trust was a wonderful experience. By the time my project came to an end in November, I had spent over 80 evenings in their presence and taken more than 100 rolls of film. The anticipation of seeing the black and white striped head of a badger emerge from its sett remained with me throughout the project, and was as strong on my last visit as it was on that very first encounter in the dark woodland theatre.

Seeing the black and white striped face of a badger emerge from sett is always a heart-stopping moment.

Oxeye daisies in Miller's Dale quarry DWT reserve

Yellow birdsnest growing on decaying leaf letter in total shade

Ox-eye daisies are also common on the quarry floor, swaying gently in the summer breeze, while the small flowers of wild thyme form a purple mat over bare ground. Many flowers act as food plants for butterflies, among them kidney vetch which is favoured by the northern brown argus, and bird's-foot trefoil, which attracts clouds of common blues. Later in the summer, grass of parnassus comes into flower. This handsome species with heart-shaped leaves and white chalice-shaped flowers is now chiefly confined to northern Britain. Its five petals are not in fact pure white but veined with translucent green stripes. At their centre nestles the glistening yellow stamens which attract bees and other pollen-transmitting insects.

Another unusual plant also finds a home along Miller's Dale. Yellow bird's-nest grows on the decaying leaves of deciduous trees, most notably beech. Unlike most other plants, yellow bird's-nest lacks chlorophyll and is therefore unable to photosynthesise using sunlight. Instead it taps into the source of nutrients provided by the decaying leaf litter, thereby enabling it to grow in deep shade without competition from other species.

Perched high above Miller's Dale and offering a superb view westwards along the dale is another DWT reserve, Priestcliffe Lees. In spring, cowslips and early purple orchids grow in profusion while in summer grass of Parnassus can be found growing alongside common spotted orchid and kidney vetch. Orange tip, green hairstreak and dingy skipper butterflies, as well as the day flying six-spot burnet moth, are also found here. The scrub layer of hawthorn, hazel and birch which divides the open grassland from the ashwoods below forms an important habitat for many breeding birds including willow warbler and blackcap. It is also the favoured habitat for dark red helleborine, a rare member of the orchid family.

The clear waters of the Wye, Lathkill and Bradford meander through several of the dales, bubbling and rushing over the limestone rocks as they wind their way towards the greater River Derwent. These rivers and streams are home to a number of plants and animals which are of national and international importance.

One species, Derbyshire feather-moss, has its only known site in the world in the White Peak, where it grows on rocks in the shallow fast-flowing water under a water-fall at a specially-protected location. The globally-threatened white-clawed crayfish is also present and otters are beginning to make a welcome comeback.

With their chestnut belly and white chest, dippers are common along stretches of fast-flowing water, where they are regularly spotted curtsying repeatedly on a rock. In places like Lathkill Dale they often become very confiding and can be watched at close quarters as they plunge kamikaze style into the rushing waters in search of food. Dippers are well adapted for this feeding strategy and are equipped with a second, thinner eyelid, which protects the eye while allowing them to chase their prey underwater.

Above: *Dark red helleborine grows well in the partially shaded scrub found on the Priestcliffe Lees DWT reserve*

Below left: *The song of willow warblers is common in hawthorn and hazel thickets*

Below right: *The dumpy form of the dipper is a regular sight along many of the Peak's fast -flowing rivers*

Dippers nest early in the year, building a substantial domed nest often under a bridge or behind a waterfall where the female can incubate her five or six eggs in relative safety. Once the chicks have hatched the male brings food to the nest and it is now that he becomes most obvious as he whizzes up and downstream. After about a week, the female joins him as they work feverishly to try to satiate their offsprings' hunger. By June, the dumpy chicks have flown the nest and begin to learn the art of underwater feeding, although they must rely on their parents for some time for a more regular food supply.

Grey wagtails gather hundreds of tiny flying insects from the water's edge to feed their chicks

The grey wagtail is a fellow inhabitant of this riverside habitat, and the two species are often encountered along the same stretch of river. Like the dipper, the grey wagtail is never still, its tail forever moving up and down in perfect rhythm with the water. Interestingly, many of the birds which inhabit these fast-flowing rivers adopt a 'bobbing' movement of some description. This may serve to help them blend in with the moving water, thereby acting as a form of camouflage.

The grey wagtail, despite its rather drab name, is a beautiful bird with bright yellow flanks and a long tail that makes it quite conspicuous as it flits restlessly from rock to rock collecting small flies. Every so often it launches energetically into flight to catch an insect in mid-air. A favoured nest site for grey wagtails is in an old wall alongside the river, such as those found holding back the waters of the old mill ponds along Bradford Dale. In the deeper water above the weir, little grebes dive for fish. Earlier in April their strange whinnying calls reverberate throughout the dale, but by summer they are busy feeding their attractively- striped chicks.

Bradford Dale is one of the best places to watch little grebes

Usually seen as a streak of cobalt blue as it flashes arrow-like over the water, a king-fisher is a thrilling sight along the rivers of the Peak District. When perched, the bright chestnut-orange underside contrasts perfectly with the dark blue wings, giving it an almost tropical appearance.

From its secluded perch, the bird dives headlong into the crystal-clear water below, expertly seizing its prey scissor-fashion in its pointed open beak. In a blur of irides-cent blue it breaks free from the water with whirring wings and returns to the perch with its prey. Minnows, sticklebacks and bullheads are the kingfisher's preferred catch. Each are despatched by repeated bashing against the branch before turning the fish so that it can be swallowed head-first, to avoid any problems with its scales or spines.

Opposite page: *The unpolluted waters of the River Lathkill provide the perfect habitat for a host of insects, birds and mammals*

Face-to-face with... Hen Harriers

During the early summer of 1997, a pair of hen harriers nested in the Goyt Valley; the first confirmed breeding success in the Peak District for 19 years. This historic event was witnessed by hundreds of bird watchers from an observation point set up by the RSPB, which undertook a round the clock vigil to protect the welcome visitors.

My first contact with the harriers followed a meeting with the site warden, Simon Travis. As we chatted, my attention was grabbed by high-pitched 'peeu peeu peeu' calls as the female rose from the nest to meet the male. Within seconds the pair performed a feat of acrobatics as the female swung underneath the male to grab the prey which her mate had brought. I was fascinated and arranged to return the next morning.

It was still dark as I made my way up the path to meet Simon but, aware of the brightening sky, we quickly headed across the moor towards the hide. The male would soon be on the wing and I could not risk him seeing me enter the hide, so as Simon wished me luck, I settled down to await my first close view of the harriers.

I didn't have to wait long. At 5.40 am the male called the female off the nest for the first food pass of the morning and seconds later he glided elegantly past the hide. It was two hours before I saw either bird again. This time the female left the nest quietly, returning a short while later with prey for her chicks. I remained in the hide until mid-afternoon, observing eight food passes and being entertained by some dramatic acrobatic displays.

Following some awful weather, I returned several days later on the promise of a fine morning from the Met office. I should have known better, for as I made my way to the hide the mist rolled in and it started to rain. Ever the optimist, I decided to set-up in the forlorn hope that the skies would clear. They didn't and so after seven damp hours, I decided to head home.

Before my next stint in the hide I erected an old fence post some distance away were I had previously seen the female perched on the ground. During my subsequent session in the hide, the usual food pass took place soon after dawn and the female flew off with the prey. Hoping to catch sight of her I peered through the hide's rear porthole and to my utter amazement I could see her posing on 'my' post!

So the following morning, I re-positioned the hide in view of the post and settled down, more in hope than expectation. But within half an hour I could make out the distinct form of a harrier gliding gently towards the post and watched spellbound as she alighted in front of me. My heart was pounding but I couldn't move a muscle for fear of alarming her. In any case the light was still too low for photography and I had to remain patient. The wait was agonising but eventually I could not resist any longer and I took a single shot – what a moment!

Over the next couple of weeks I spent more than 100 hours in the hide and was fortunate to obtain a series of images of the female harrier. By the end of July the chicks were exercising their wings above the nest and a few days later I watched them flying tentatively over the moor in pursuit of the male, who continued to feed them for some time. The female had left the moor earlier and eventually all four chicks dispersed along with the handsome grey male.

Despite high hopes, the harriers did not return the following year and, largely as a result of persecution, they remain a very rare breeding bird throughout England, raising fears of the future of these spectacular moorland predators.

A female hen harrier alights on a post with prey – my favourite picture from this project

An experienced bird can expect to catch a fish on every second or third dive, but the newly-fledged youngsters fare less well and many drown before they have mastered the technique. Fishing is often followed by preening, an activity of vital importance to maintain the feathers in good condition. A good deal of time is dedicated to this activity, and a bird will make repeated short dives interspersed with lengthy bouts of preening.

Kingfishers are only found where there are steep-sided riverbanks in which they can excavate their small nesting chamber up to a metre into the bank. In early spring the pair will hurl themselves at the banking using their sharp beaks to form the beginnings of a hole. It may take them many days of hard digging before the tunnel is complete by which time the pair will have mated, ready for egg laying.

This preference for nesting in riverbanks is shared by sand martins. These summer visitors nest in small colonies along the River Derwent where they can be seen flying low over the water in search of insects.

Goosanders are becoming more numerous on several of the Peak's rivers

At one time, kingfishers were the scourge of fisherman who believed they were in direct competition. This unfortunate reputation has now been taken by the goosander, a species that is on the increase along several of the Peak's rivers. Goosanders are accomplished at the art of underwater fishing, a skill that has made them unpopular with some anglers. These large ducks are handsome birds. The male has a bottle green head and pinkish tinge to his mainly white breast. The female by contrast has a brown head with a distinctive crest.

In the spring, the pair may be seen prospecting for a suitable nest site in a hollow tree, but once the female is tucked away inside the drake disappears altogether and takes no further part in family affairs. The delightful, fluffy brown and white chicks hatch in summer and leave the nest after only a few days.

The female leaves the nest first and calls to them from the water below. One by one the ducklings move to the entrance of the nest hole and throw themselves into mid-air, tumbling down on stunted wings to join their mother. The family remains together for several weeks. During this time she leads them over great distances, negotiating small waterfalls and rapids along their territory. This is a dangerous time for the chicks as they can easily become separated from their mother and are more likely to fall victim to the fearsome pike or some other predator.

A male kingfisher with his catch ready to deliver to his chicks in a nearby riverbank

Otters were absent from the Peak District for many years but thankfully are now making a comeback

The otter is also on the increase, making a welcome comeback along several river systems. They have already re-established themselves in low numbers along the Dove and Lower Derwent and will hopefully continue to recolonise many of their former haunts. The Otters and Rivers Project, a joint initiative between the Wildlife Trusts, the Environment Agency and Severn Trent Water, is working to provide otters with the kind of habitat that they require by restoring riverside habitat as well as installing a number of artificial holts.

Severn Trent Water play a key role in this project, not only in terms of providing the necessary funding but also in their role as riparian landowners. By the nature of their business, Severn Trent Water own large tracts of land alongside rivers. These consist of many quiet areas, some of which have been fenced off and left completely undisturbed. These places, together with water treatment works, provide valuable habitat which otters moving into the Peak will hopefully be able to exploit in the future.

Otters are generally shy, solitary animals and are active mainly at night, which makes them difficult to observe. As a result, much of the Otter Project's monitoring work involves scanning riverbanks looking for spraints (droppings), a positive indicator of an otter's presence. Each individual leaves its own personal 'calling card' on prominent rocks and logs. These markers provide other otters with important information, in particular the sex of the owner and, if it's a female, whether she is in season.

The female lives separately from the dog otter apart from the few days when she is ready to mate. When she is ready, she retreats to find a quiet place where she gives birth to her cubs. Most otter cubs are born in spring and they remain with their mother for between 10-14 months. During this time she will provide them with a rich supply of milk and a regular supply of fish and other prey. As they reach adulthood, the young otters spend a great deal of their time honing their hunting skills as they practise the art of fishing under the expert guidance of their mother.

The good news that otters are back is testament to the inherent survival mechanism of these creatures. Their resurgence also serves as an indicator that the region's rivers are becoming more suitable as a wildlife habitat. The otter's return is welcome news for another of the region's most threatened mammals, the water vole. These delightful creatures, immortalised as Ratty in Kenneth Grahame's famous tales of The Wind in the Willows, have been disappearing from the Peak's waterways at an alarming rate. One of the chief reasons for this decline is the increased numbers of mink that originally escaped from fur farms and have subsequently established themselves throughout most of the country.

Mink are ferocious predators and are small enough to enter the bankside burrows of water voles, killing their young and decimating the vole population. They are also nomadic and will leave a territory once they have raided the larder, moving on to look for a fresh food supply. Otters however will not tolerate mink in their territory and will drive them out or even kill them. This effectively removes the water voles' main predator and restores the natural order to the riverbank.

Although they have decreased in overall population, water voles are still a common sight along Lathkill Dale where they can be surprisingly tame. Early morning and late afternoon are good times of the day to watch for them. Look for their characteristic burrows in the riverbank as well as for areas of recently nibbled vegetation close by. During the summer a patient wait at one of these sites should be rewarded with some good views of young water voles which join the adults to nibble their way through clumps of reeds and sedges.

The Peak District remains one of the best places in the country to see water voles

A red fox licks its lips in anticipation of its next meal

Like the mink, the rabbit was once high on the country's most hated list for its destructive habits. But this wasn't always the case. Introduced from continental Europe by the Normans, rabbits were highly-prized for their pelts and meat. They were originally bred in captivity but they inevitably escaped from their enclosed warrens and gradually established themselves in the open countryside. They are now accepted as part of the British countryside, although their liking for vegetables makes them unpopular with some gardeners.

Rabbits are common throughout the Peak District, favouring the open pastures of the White Peak but also present along the moorland fringes. Early summer sees the emergence of the youngsters. Far less wary than the adults, these miniature versions of their parents can be watched at close quarters as they pop up and bound out from their burrows during the early evening. They often congregate with siblings and near neighbours forming little gangs outside their communal homes.

Periodically, the young rabbits return to the warm soil outside their burrows where they sit around and indulge in periods of grooming. Siblings may rub noses as a form of greeting and often play together in the warmth of a summer's evening. As dusk approaches the entire clan will be busily munching buttercup stalks and grass stems, an activity that will continue throughout the short summer night. By dawn, wet from the overnight dew, most will find a warm sunny position to dry off their coats. Left undisturbed, they will remain above ground for much of the morning, but at the first hint of danger, the alarm is raised and they all scamper for the safety of their burrows.

In contrast to many introduced species, rabbits have a number of natural predators. Foxes, stoats, weasels and buzzards have all benefited from their presence and for some, rabbits form the largest part of their diet. Indeed, during the early 1950's when the rabbit population was so badly blighted by the myxomatosis virus, some of these predatory species suffered a similar decline. Although periodic cases of myxomatosis still occur, the rabbit population is once again very buoyant, providing predators with a ready source of prey throughout the summer months.

In the long grass meadows of the White Peak, the fox stealthily approaches its prey, remaining undetected by the rabbit's twitching nose and ears. Then, from just a few metres away, the fox explodes from cover to quickly despatch its victim. However, if spotted the rabbit's speed and agility is able to out-run the fox and it must move on to new ground in search of a meal. The stoat is equally effective in its hunting

technique. These ruthless killers employ a different strategy to that of the fox, but the result is invariably the same. For the rabbit, death from an attack by a stoat can be a terrible ordeal.

One cunning ploy used by a hunting stoat is to run rapidly in tight circles around its prey, mesmerising the unfortunate victim and allowing the stoat to leap for its neck. Despite its small size (an adult male is 30cm in length), a stoat is a fearsome predator, capable of killing a rabbit six times heavier than itself. Active both day and night, it relentlessly tracks down its prey by scent. Occasionally the rabbit being hunted will become panic-stricken and will simply lie down and squeal loudly as the stoat approaches.

Stoats mate in the summer but implantation of the fertilised egg is delayed until the following March so that the female can give birth in spring to coincide with the abundance of prey. Females make their dens in rock crevices, hollow trees or old rabbit burrows, where they give birth to six or more young. The young leave the den after around five weeks and the family party often play together in summer, leading to the misconception that they hunt in packs.

Weasels are similar in appearance to stoats although they are much smaller and have a short tail, whereas that of the stoat is long with a black tip. Weasels sometimes stand upright to give themselves a better field of view, showing off their pale undersides. More often they move in undulating bounds, gracefully covering the ground, although when required they can run with astonishing speed. The weasel's main prey is mice and voles which they find in abundance in the meadows and rough grasslands of the Peak.

Above left: *Stoats are ferocious predators which hunt rabbits, voles, mice and birds*

Above right: *Both stoats and weasels (pictured here) utilise dry stone walls to ambush their prey*

Relict of the Past or a Bright Future?

Traditional flower-rich hay meadows, with their intimate mix of grasses and herbs, are a valuable resource for wildlife. Ecologically, the most interesting meadows are those which are long-established, with each field having developed its own unique range of plants which may include crested dogtail, sheep fescue, sorrel, hay rattle, meadow vetchlng, common knapweed, meadow buttercup, field scabious and ox-eye daisy. In addition, they are important habitats for breeding birds such as skylark, lapwing and curlew while also providing an essential feeding habitat for twite, a bird of national significance.

Once a common sight throughout the Peak District, good quality hay meadows have become increasingly rare. The Hay Meadows Project set up by the National Park Authority in late 1994, surveyed a total of 959 meadows and found that the majority had been subject to a degree of agricultural improvement with only 13 per cent remaining of a high quality. A comparison with earlier data indicated a 50 per cent loss in flower-rich meadows between the 1930s and mid 1980s and a further 26 per cent decline in the proceeding decade.

Through a process of co-operation with farmers and landowners, the work of the HMP resulted in 151 of the surveyed hay meadows being entered into conservation agreements. Furthermore, many of the Peak's most important hay meadows are designated as SSSIs, including Rose End Meadows, Bradwell Meadows, Lee Farm Meadow and meadows within the Leek Moors SSSI. The National Park Authority and the National Trust also own significant hay meadows, for example at Monyash and in the Upper Derwent, while the Wildlife Trusts manage other key sites.

Hay meadow conservation is an on-going project, and English Nature has recently undertaken meadow restoration trials in five fields adjacent to the Derbyshire Dales National Nature Reserve in Lathkill Dale. These fields have been treated as pasture for many years although they are presumed to have been hay meadows in the past.

The aim is to use the site as a demonstration area to encourage farmers and landowners to consider species-rich hay meadows as an alternative to botanically poor silage fields. This work also forms part of the Peak District Biodiversity Action Plan that has set a target to restore 20 ha of flower rich hay meadow by 2010.

Restoration work began in 1999 when the fields were first cut for hay and was followed by a positive management of grazing, thistle control, harrowing and wild flower seed application, most notably hay rattle sourced locally from long-standing hay meadows.

One of the aims of this trial is to formulate an appropriate management scheme for other similar projects, but perhaps the biggest challenge for the future is the need to "sell" the value and benefits of traditional species-rich meadows to landowners and farmers. With many meadows still unprotected they remain at risk of being switched to silage production and may be lost forever.

For the sake of the profusion of wild plants and animals which find refuge within these treasured places, continued action is required to ensure that the Peak's remaining hay meadows have a bright future and are not simply memories of a bygone age.

Traditional flower-rich meadows can still be found in the White Peak

If you are lucky enough to have one of these inquisitive creatures in view try making a squeaking noise by 'kissing' the back of your hand. Both stoats and weasels have a lively curiosity and may come closer to investigate or at least stop in their tracks long enough for you to get a proper look.

The summer grasslands and hay meadows which provide sustenance for the countless mice and voles reach their floral peak during June and July. Vivid yellow meadow buttercups shimmer in the breeze alongside meadow saxifrage and oxeye daisy. In the centuries-old traditional hay meadows, yellow rattle grows with greater knapweed, field scabious and adder's tongue, a specialist fern of unimproved meadows. These flower-rich meadows support a wealth of insect life including the hill cuckoo bee, an important indicator species of this ancient habitat.

The breeding success of the twite, an unobtrusive small brown finch, is wholly dependent on the availability of wildflower seed on which they exclusively feed their chicks. For this reason, twite invariably nest close to hay meadows or other plentiful supplies of seeds. This unusual feature of the twite's lifestyle has led to its decline over the past few decades, with a decrease of 50 per cent recorded in the Peak during the 1990s. The UK as a whole has 99 per cent of the European twite population with the vast majority (10,000 pairs) in western Scotland. The English population of between 250 and 500 pairs is found only in the southern Pennines, making the twite a true Peak District speciality.

Above: *The Peak District provides important habitat for breeding twite*

Right: *The bright yellow fields of meadow buttercups are a vivid reminder of traditional farming methods*

A little owl pauses at the entrance to its nest site

The drystone walls that surround the hay meadows provide nest sites for little owls, a species introduced into Britain in the late nineteenth century. These small owls are hole nesters and may choose to nest in a hollow tree or an old rabbit burrow, but a cavity within a drystone wall serves them equally well. Here the pair will raise their brood of two or three chicks on a plentiful supply of beetles, earthworms, moths and the occasional vole or shrew.

Little owls are diurnal and can sometimes be spotted perched near the nest site, basking in the early morning sunshine. During the middle of the day they tend to retreat to a quiet place to roost but they may be disturbed by other birds that become agitated by their presence, noisily mobbing the predator until it moves away. As dusk approaches they become active once again, utilising the fading light to hunt more easily. During this twilight period the pair will catch as much prey as possible for their chicks. After a few weeks, the chicks, now resembling fluffy balls of feathers, wait eagerly at the entrance of the nest for their parents' return.

The Longdendale Trail, which follows the old line of the Manchester to Sheffield railway, was designed to provide an attractive route through the valley for cyclists, walkers and horse riders, but it has also become a haven for butterflies. The tall

The Longdendale Trail is a wonderful place for butterflies, including the dark green fritillary

railway embankments provide good shelter from the wind and the diversity of plants and flowers has proved to be very attractive for a range of butterflies. In total, 19 species have been recorded, including the dark green fritillary and brimstone.

As part of the original landscaping scheme, many flowers were planted, including birds foot trefoil which serves as the food plant for the common blue. Tiny green hairstreak butterflies can be found on the widespread bilberry, while the bright purple flower heads of thistles attracts red admiral, peacock, painted lady and small tortoiseshell. Commas can be found on bramble, a plant which also attracts gate-keepers to its flowers. This species, also known as hedge brown, was absent from the southern Pennines until recently, but may now be seen dancing along hedgerows on warm summer days.

Small colonies of purple hairstreaks have also recently been discovered in Longdendale's small woods, such as the Brockholes Wood Nature Reserve. This woodland species is associated with oaks and is perhaps best seen by lying on your back and staring up into the canopy, where you may catch a glimpse of this small butterfly fluttering through the trees.

Purple is certainly the over-riding colour high on the heather moors of the Dark Peak during August when the often bleak moorlands are transformed by swathes of colour. A sea of purple stretches into the distance, guiding the eye over a patchwork of heather which is punctuated only by the many rocky gritstone tors.

Mid-August heralds a transformation of Burbage Moors as the heather comes into flower

Above: *Cross-leaved heath prefers wet moorland*

Above right: *The vivid purple flowers of bell heather are at their best in July*

Below: *Ling is the commonest and most widespread of the heathers*

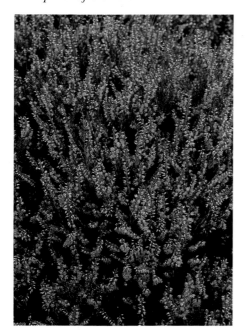

These are the heady days of summer, a time when residents and visitors alike can enjoy the flowering expanses of heather and breathe in the intoxicating smell of pollen wafting up from the purple flowers. The air is alive with the constant buzzing of bees as they move from flower to flower feeding on the sweet nectar. Most will be honey bees which come to feast upon this short-lived bounty, although some may be visitors, brought in for the annual harvest by local bee-keepers.

Although usually referred to simply as heather, there are three distinct species found in the Peak's moorland habitat. The commonest and most widespread is ling, a name that derives from the Norse word 'lig' meaning fire, with which moorland habitat has always had a close relationship. In some of the boggy areas of the moors, cross-leaved heath covers the wet peat. It can be identified by its clusters of lilac-coloured, lantern-like flowers. By contrast, bell heather is vivid purple and favours the drier parts of the moors, where it flowers much earlier in the summer.

Other classic moorland plants include the ubiquitous bilberry as well as cowberry and crowberry, all of which produce small sweet fruits which are consumed by many of the migratory birds before they fly south. Carpets of cottongrass cover many of the wetter areas of the moors, their fluffy white heads swaying rhythmically in the breeze. Early in the summer the bright yellow spikes of bog asphodel decorate the sides of moorland pools. Blanket bog specialists such as bog rosemary and Labrador tea can also be found growing in small numbers, and other unusual species include the carnivorous insect-trapping plants, such as round-leaved sundew and butterwort

A sea of cotton grass sways gently in the breeze near Stanage Edge

Mini-lobsters Return

Until relatively recently, the white-clawed crayfish was a commonplace lobster-like inhabitant of most rivers throughout the Peak District. However over the past two decades, its population has been decimated largely as a consequence of the arrival of an alien species of crayfish brought over from America to stock rivers for the crayfish meat market.

The American signal crayfish is substantially bigger than our native crayfish, with bright red claws and an aggressive attitude. It is able to out-compete the white-clawed crayfish for food and even preys on it; two factors that have led to the decline of our native species.

Even more sinister was the fact that signal crayfish brought with it crayfish plague, an infection which is fatal to white-clawed crayfish. Signal crayfish are immune to the disease but act as carriers, releasing the infection on spores that are spread through the water system. Entire populations of white-clawed crayfish have been lost as a result including that of the River Wye, where the species disappeared over a five-year period in the early 1990s.

The River Lathkill population was also wiped out by the plague which was probably carried in by fish coming into the river from another catchment area. However, once the native crayfish population had been lost and with no signal crayfish on which to survive, the disease soon died out. In fact, no other environmental changes had taken place on the Lathkill. The habitat and water quality remained the same; the only things missing were the white-clawed crayfish. This set of circumstances prompted English Nature to undertake a re-introduction programme in an attempt to re-establish a viable breeding population.

Twenty white-clawed crayfish were subsequently taken from a separate thriving population for the re-introduction. There was little point in simply releasing this small number into the River Lathkill as it might be many years before any detectable increase in population occurred. Instead, a captive breeding programme was established in order to quickly build up the numbers.

Each female can produce around 50 eggs which cling on to her underside. They hatch in May and June and have the appearance of miniature replicas of the adults but are only 1mm in length. They are unusual creatures in that as they grow, they moult, discarding their old casing and upgrading to a new home.

The juveniles remain in special containers sunk into the bed of the River Lathkill until they are between one and two years old and have had three or four moults. At this stage most are then released into areas of the river where there is less likelihood of predation from brown trout. The remaining juveniles are retained for further breeding.

Several hundred young crayfish have been released into the river since the project began in 1997 with funding from the EU. The release site in Lathkill Dale is a long way from rival signal crayfish populations, so it is hoped that the white-clawed population will continue to flourish and that this re-introduction programme may serve as a case study for other similar projects in the future.

The native white-clawed crayfish seen here has been decimated by non-native signal crayfish introduced from America

Above: *Round-leaved sundew traps its prey on sweet-tasting sticky goblets*

Right: *The red grouse is a denizen of the heather moors of the Dark Park*

A female merlin perched close to her nest

Heather moorland is the principal domain of Britain's most highly-prized game bird, the red grouse. These plump birds eke out a meagre existence, depending almost exclusively on heather for food, shelter and a place to nest. After braving the winter storms, the males begin to set up breeding territories in early spring, proclaiming their presence with unmistakable 'go-back, go-back, go-back' calls. As spring advances, the tender new heather shoots provide the pair with vital food. During this time they remain close together, the male spending much of his time defending his territory, while the female is busy feeding.

Once the eggs are laid much of the activity subsides, but by early June, the broods of chicks are beginning to hatch out in synchrony across the moors. The chicks are mobile soon after hatching and almost immediately begin to peck away at the heather and pick off insects. The chicks remain with both parents for several weeks and can still be seen in family parties at onset of the shooting season on 'the Glorious Twelfth' of August.

Another moorland specialist is the impressive looking emperor moth, complete with striking eyespots on its wings. Ling is the main larval food plant for their attractive green and black caterpillars which can often be seen in late summer moving along bare footpaths. The adult moths fly by day and provide food for the fast flying merlin. This small agile falcon hawks low over the heather preying upon these large insects, which it catches with amazing dexterity. Its chief prey however, is small birds, particularly the meadow pipits that breed in high densities right across the uplands.

Peregrine falcons are capable of speeds of over 300kph as they swoop onto their prey

By late summer whinchats can be seen hunting for insects among the heather, regularly hopping down onto the ground to seize a juicy caterpillar. The chicks accompany their parents for some time after leaving the nest but soon they will leave the moors and head south to the coast as they begin their journey back to Africa. But for now the whinchats and other migrants may tempt an inexperienced peregrine to try its luck. The young falcons must quickly learn to fend for themselves, and an unwary juvenile whinchat may allow a peregrine to hone its skills.

The fortunes of the peregrine have fluctuated over the years. Deforestation by our ancestors favoured these falcons, as they prefer to hunt over open ground. But the advent of game shooting caused their demise during the Victorian era when many were persecuted along with all other predators that were deemed to interfere with game species. During the Second World War, peregrines suffered a further set back as over 600 were destroyed to prevent them killing carrier pigeons bringing back important messages. The population recovered after the war and they were fully protected in all areas by the Protection of Birds Act of 1954.

However, a more sinister fate was yet to befall the species. During 1961-2, the British Trust for Ornithology carried out a national survey of peregrine breeding grounds. Alarmingly out of 500 known nesting sites only 250 were occupied and of these only a quarter produced any young. There was clearly something wrong.

Further investigation identified organo-chlroine pesticides, introduced in the 1940s and '50s, as the problem. These highly toxic chemicals entered the food chain and accumulated in peregrines, killing both old and young. These pesticides also caused a reduction in the thickness of the eggshells, resulting in breakage and infertility. DDT and dieldrin were found to be the main problems and were later banned from use in the UK. Fortunately, peregrine numbers have subsequently recovered. In the Peak District they mostly nest on cliff ledges as well as quarry faces, where they will happily raise a brood surrounded by the commotion of the working site below.

Once the heather seed has ripened in early September, other species flock to the moors to feed. Family parties of bullfinches and linnets call and twitter as they fly overhead in search of the ripest seeds. The male of both these species has a delightful pink chest which perfectly complements the last flush of colour from the heather. Twite and other finches also cash in on this annual harvest and may form large roving flocks.

Alport Castles provides an ideal site for peregrines

On late summer mornings common lizards bask on rocks in exposed sites among the heather. The warming rays of sun slowly raises their body temperature, releasing them from their overnight stupor so that they can begin to hunt insects. Some moorlands also support small populations of adders, Britain's only poisonous snake, which preys on lizards as well as mice and voles. They are secretive creatures which are able to detect their prey, as well as an approaching human, through vibrations in the ground. Consequently, more often than not they slink away into the heather where their cryptic diamond patterning makes them much harder to see.

On face value the impoverished acidic soil of the moors seems an unlikely habitat in which this diversity of wildlife is able to flourish. For the most part it is the heather that provides the key link in the chain. But this is not the whole story, for another crucial component lies hidden underground in the form of a fungus which associates specifically with the roots of the heather, providing the plant with the essential nutrients that allow it to thrive.

From humble beginnings the Dark Peak moors have become an integral part of the Peak District landscape, and while they can be hostile, unwelcoming places at times, for a few weeks at least they reveal their softer side, delighting visitors with a glorious floral climax to the high days of summer.

Above left: *The female common lizard is predominantly brown compared to the green male*

Above right: *Adders are seldom seen moorland inhabitants due to their cryptic markings and shy nature*

Chapter 4
AUTUMN
Mists and Mellow Fruitfulness

The departure of the swifts is the first indication that summer has come to an end. These remarkable birds are the briefest of visitors to our shores, arriving from Africa in late April and returning during September. At the end of their breeding season, large numbers can be seen circling high in the sky as they feed spectacularly on the wing before heading south for the winter. Earlier in the summer their weird screeching calls reverberate through many of the Peak's towns and villages as they return to their traditional nesting sites.

The swift's dark form and long pointed wings are unmistakable as it slices through the air at great speed, catching insects to fuel its never-ending aerial stunts. Swifts spend almost their entire lives on the wing, eating, drinking and even sleeping while in the air. It is only during the brief nesting season that the adults come back to earth, crawling through small gaps in buildings to raise their young in attics, old mills, factories and churches. But once their parental duties are complete they depart, vanishing overnight as quickly as they arrived.

Similar in shape to swifts, house martins and swallows belong to a separate family called Hirundines. House martins are chiefly urban dwellers, securing their nest of mud to the underside of the eaves of houses where they may raise up to three broods of chicks. Together with swallows they hawk over the meadows and pastures of the Peak District long after the swifts have departed, collecting flying insects in their gaping mouths.

Swallows also rely on buildings, preferring to nest in barns and stables to which generation after generation have returned each spring. They are common throughout the Peak District, although a reduction in older buildings and the modernisation of some farms has left them with a smaller number of nesting sites. In early autumn they gather in large numbers on overhead wires and are often joined by house martins. Here they spend their time preening and chattering noisily as they prepare themselves for the long flight back across the Sahara.

A young swift displays its wide gape that helps it to catch insects on the wing

Swallows rely on old farm buildings in which they can build their nest of mud and straw

Opposite page: *Unused millstones litter the Bole Hill birchwoods under Millstone Edge*

Right: *Common blue damselflies display their unique mating pose*

Far right: *A common darter at rest*

Goldfinches are equipped with slender bills which allow them to probe deep into the teasel head to extract the tiny seeds

Just as the swallows and martins gather together in autumn so do many of our resident birds. Goldfinches form small parties called 'charms' which flock to feed on the seed heads of thistles and teasels and delight us with their musical, twittering calls. Their long pointed bills are perfectly adapted to prize the deep seated seeds from within the protected spines of the teasel head. Their charms may be joined by greenfinches that also revel in tearing apart the fluffy seed heads of thistles. The discarded feathery parachutes drift gently on the breeze, as the birds deftly remove the seeds.

Several species of damselfly and dragonfly flit with equal grace over many of the region's pools throughout the early part of autumn The dazzling beauty of dragonflies belies their predatory skills both as an adult and as a larva. On close inspection, dragonflies have huge compound eyes which they use to track down their prey in flight, often returning to a favoured perch to consume their meal. Underwater, the larva employ a more leisurely but equally effective technique for catching prey. Moving slowly to within a few centimetres of an unsuspecting victim, the larva suddenly shoots out its claws to grasp its prey which it then devours methodically.

As the autumn equinox approaches, great changes begin to take place in the countryside, triggered by an ever-decreasing number of daylight hours and a gradual drop in temperature. Following spells of clear weather, warm Indian summer days are followed by overnight frosts and cool damp mornings. Dew-covered orb spiders' webs sparkle like jewels in the sunshine of daybreak and the meadows are glistening with the millions of water droplets which have accumulated on grasses.

Many plants and flowers have already set seed and withered away before autumn, but some of the late flowering summer species continue to put on a show throughout September and into October. The nodding blue heads of harebells are a common sight in the limestone dales where they grow alongside knapweed, field scabious and hawkweed. Grass of Parnassus, a beautiful, honey-scented plant, produces its delicate white flowers in late summer and may still be found in full display in early autumn. Traditionally, a flower of marshy moorland fringes, this now-localised plant can be found at several sites along Miller's Dale.

Above: *Harebells continue to flower well into autumn*

Left: *The dew-covered webs of garden spiders sparkle in the early morning sun*

Face-to-face with... Red Deer

Travelling through the suburbs of Disley to the south of Manchester, I was having great difficulty imagining a wild rugged moorland landscape where red deer roamed. As I arrived at Lyme Park in the twilight of an October dawn I was greeted with the sight of a large stately home but few signs of the wilder side of this impressive National Trust estate.

This all changed as I left the warm confines of my car and stepped into the cool, damp autumnal air. Away in the distance I could hear the deep bass sounds of a red deer stag bellowing and more distantly, a second stag roaring his defiant response.

With no prior knowledge of the park, I headed out in the direction from where the roars were emanating. The concrete and traffic of south Manchester was soon forgotten as I made my way across the bracken-covered moorland. Within a few hundred metres of the car park, I came across two young stags who eyed me suspiciously before trotting off out of sight. Photographing these shy creatures was going to be more difficult than I had been led to believe, and I would have to be stealthier if I was going to get close enough for good photographs.

Stalking any wild animal is never easy. Their heightened sense of smell and acute hearing gives them a distinct advantage over us humans who are equipped only with good eyesight. Red deer like many mammals can pick up a human scent from great distance, especially on damp mornings when our body odours hang in the air. The slightest breeze can carry these tell-tale scents over several hundred metres, so it was paramount that any approach I made was with the wind blowing directly in my face to help carry away my scent.

I could still hear the two stags bellowing, so I continued to walk slowly towards them. Eventually I was rewarded with a good view of one of them and I could clearly see him strutting arrogantly around his 'patch', watched keenly by several hinds. From his demeanour and the number of hinds within his harem it was apparent that this was one of the dominant stags. By using the bracken as cover and making a careful approach towards the group I was able to find a good vantage point.

After watching and photographing the deer for a few minutes I attempted to move closer – big mistake! One of the hinds spotted me and immediately stamped the ground to alert the rest of the group. I remained motionless hoping that the deer would realise that I posed no threat.

After a while the hinds, still aware by my presence, began to drift slowly away but the stag and a few females remained close-by. He was clearly not going to move until he had rounded up the remaining hinds. This gave me the opportunity I had been waiting for and, as the stag and the two last hinds reached the top of a small ridge, I obtained my favourite shot of the morning – the stag silhouetted against a stormy autumnal sky.

A red deer stag pauses momentarily before disappearing from view

Above: *Cowberry and other berry-laden moorland plants attract thrushes in autumn*

Above right: *Rowan berries are highly sought after by fieldfares and redwings*

While the seed heads of many plants provide finches and tits with a plentiful supply of food, the moorlands of the Dark Peak are also a rich source of food for upland birds. The small dark berries of bilberry and crowberry as well as the red fruits of cowberry are a welcome treat for the remaining flocks of ring ouzels. Unfortunately for the birds, the much scarcer cloudberry, a subalpine shrub found on some moors, rarely bears fruit due to an overwhelming preponderance of male plants.

The rowan, or mountain ash as it is often referred to because of its preference for the uplands, is bedecked with clusters of bright red berries from the onset of autumn. This early fruiting makes it popular with many birds. Ring ouzels, blackbirds, song thrushes and mistle thrushes all flock to feast on the ripening berries, with territorial skirmishes taking place over the most favoured trees. Mistle thrushes can be particularly aggressive and a single bird may defend an entire rowan from intruders, chasing would-be rivals away with vicious attacks.

By mid-September the bramble, much revered for its thorny stems and invasive nature, shows its softer side. Along the hedgerows and field margins wildlife and humans feed upon the succulent, dark purple blackberries with equal enthusiasm. Magpies, jays and wood pigeons as well as thrushes and finches all descend to cash in on these highly-prized autumnal offerings. Small mammals such as bank voles and wood mice climb the thorny stems and hang acrobatically as they pluck the tasty morsels from their stalks. Badgers, foxes and even hedgehogs are also tempted to join the feasting, stripping the outer berries and helping to disperse the seeds far and wide.

Opposite page: *A bank vole quietly nibbles on ripening blackberries*

Above: *Hawthorn berries provide field-fares with a much-needed supply of food during periods of frost*

Above right: *Nuthatches feed on a wide source of food and will regularly visit garden peanut feeders*

As the autumn progresses a succession of food becomes available. Berries from the elder, holly and hawthorn add to the diversity of fruits on offer along the hedgerows and woodland edges. As each crop ripens birds move in to enjoy this short-lived banquet. Flocks of wood pigeons systematically strip the elderberries, while black-caps and other lingering warblers flit about the branches, selectively picking off the juiciest fruits. These are joined by starlings, blackbirds and other thrushes, all unable to resist the sweet fruits that hang heavy on the slender branches.

For many birds and animals autumn is not simply a matter of enjoying the variations on the menu, but it is more importantly a time when they can lay down extra reserves which will help them survive the winter. Even for some of the summer migrants, the fruits of autumn play a vital role in their survival. In order to make their arduous journeys back to Africa they must gain extra fat as a source of energy, and to help them do this they gorge themselves on berries and other available foods.

During this crucial time of the year there can be a great deal of competition for food. The resident birds and the remaining summer migrants may have the best of the rich pickings, but as autumn progresses the first influx of winter visitors arrive from the continent. Redwings and fieldfares as well as continental blackbirds and thrushes descend on berry-laden trees throughout the Peak District. Their relatively short journey across the North Sea is rewarded with a much-needed energy boost as they flock to the hawthorns and rowans soon after their arrival.

Each autumn's harvest is different and, while there is always a reasonable supply of food, some seasons are much better than others. In some years the hedgerows may be laden with fruits while in others there is hardly a berry to be seen. These natural fluctuations have a direct and noticeable effect on the populations of some species. Redwings and fieldfares, present throughout the Peak District whenever there is a bumper crop of haws and other berries, are largely absent in poor fruiting years. Although preferring to feed on worms and other live food, the winter thrushes rely on a good supply of berries to help see them through periods of cold weather when the ground is frozen hard, trapping potential food below the hard crust.

While the vast majority of the berries are usually quickly consumed once they ripen, the nuts and seeds are longer-lasting and help to ensure a regular supply of food throughout the autumn and in some cases well into winter. One of the most widespread is the acorn, an important source of energy for many woodland species, including the nuthatch. These colourful birds wedge acorns into crevices in the bark and then use their powerful beaks to crack open the tough outer casing to get at the nutritious nut inside.

Jays have an even greater passion for acorns, gorging themselves throughout the autumn. These attractive members of the crow family are much in evidence at this time of the year, their bright blue wing patches showing superbly as they fly from tree to tree. In years that provide a plentiful supply of acorns, several jays may be seen feeding together under well-stocked oaks. Although each jay consumes great numbers of acorns during the autumn, they often bury far more than they eat in order to provide them with a much needed source of food during the leaner winter months.

The jay is the most colourful member of the crow family, with a penchant for acorns

Face-to-face with... Fieldfares and Redwings

The arrival of autumn is seen most emphatically by the dramatically-changing colours of the leaves on the trees. But in the birding world, it is the sound of the fieldfares and redwings which I find most symbolic of the season.

The magical 'chack-chack' calls of flocks of fieldfares as they pass overhead is for me the epitome of autumn, just as the call of the cuckoo symbolises the spring. These northern thrushes arrive on our north-eastern shores from Scandinavia and quickly make their way south and west, usually arriving in the Peak District in late September.

At first they may go largely unnoticed as they feed alongside mistle thrushes in open fields searching for earthworms. But as the mornings grow colder and the first frosts of autumn begin to take hold, so fieldfares and their smaller cousins, the redwings, seek out berry-laden hawthorns and rowans. It had always been an ambition of mine to capture this seasonal activity on film and despite several previous attempts my results were frankly pitiful.

My earlier efforts were based largely on a haphazard approach of erecting a portable hide facing a well-stocked hawthorn hedge where I had seen fieldfares feeding and hoping that they would return. While this technique had some merits and did yield a few reasonable pictures, the strike rate was very low and often birds would feed tantalisingly close but just out of view or too high in the hedge. From my static fixed position I had very little leeway and unless the birds landed in the exact spot in front of the hide I was unable to get a shot.

After a few attempts, I realised that there had to be an easier way. So I began driving around the Peak District searching for hawthorn hedgerows which were close to a roadside where I could park safely. Once located, I returned to these hedgerows frequently to check to see if any birds were feeding. The timing of this was critical for I knew that fieldfares search out the ripest berries and that they can quickly strip a hedgerow once they get started. I also required good sunlight falling directly onto the hedge if I was to obtain brightly-lit pictures.

Eventually, all these factors came together and for two frosty November days, I was able to photograph fieldfares, redwings and blackbirds feeding enthusiastically on the juicy haws. The car effectively served as a mobile photographic hide towards which the birds showed no concern, as presumably they were well-accustomed to seeing vehicles drive by their dining area. From the car I was quickly able to establish where the birds perched most often and where they favoured to feed. I could also see the berries disappearing and was able to re-position the car so that I was close to the last remaining berries.

Using the vehicle in this way worked exceptionally well for this type of photography and gave me the flexibility that I needed to record these attractive birds, as they indulged in their annual pilgrimage to the region's well-stocked hedgerows.

Redwings join other thrushes to feast on hawthorn berries in cold weather

The grey squirrel's ability to feed on unripened acrons gives it a clear advantage over the native red squirrel

The jay's strategy is mirrored by grey squirrels who use their front feet to dig small holes in which to conceal their prized acorns. While jays may well rely on memory to retrieve their buried treasure, it is more likely that the grey squirrels use their acute sense of smell to re-locate theirs. Despite their skills of recollection, the many oak seedlings that sprout from the woodland floor each spring is testament to the limitations of both species.

The grey squirrel's ability to eat acorns and other foods before they are fully ripe puts them at a distinct advantage over many of its avian competitors, and more significantly, the native red squirrel, a species that is now sadly believed to be absent from the Peak District. In the recent past red squirrels were a regular sight in many of the coniferous woodlands, but it seems that they have now lost their tenuous foothold altogether.

The reason for their demise lies largely at the door of the grey squirrel, a species introduced from North America in the 1870s. One of the first documented releases was in 1876 near Macclesfield, and they subsequently spread into the Peak District during the 1930s and today are widespread throughout most corners of the Park.

Red squirrel populations had historically fluctuated as a consequence of food availability, but it was the introduction and spread of the grey squirrel that led to their steady decline. While red squirrels are specialised feeders, unable to fully digest acorns or green hazelnuts, greys are more general feeders and have the advantage of being able to eat unripened hazelnuts and acorns. Grey squirrels are also significantly larger than reds and are able to compete for food more effectively. They are also believed to be responsible for transmitting the viral disease parapox (to which they are immune) to red squirrels, causing many infected animals to die.

As the red squirrel population declined throughout the Peak District, grey squirrels continued to thrive, raiding bird tables and escalating in numbers in most areas. With few natural predators and the ability to produce two litters of young each year, the grey squirrel – known to farmers and foresters as 'tree-rats' – is here to stay, whether we like it or not. Unfortunately, the same cannot be said for the red squirrel unless unpopular measures are taken to cull grey squirrels in certain areas in order to facilitate a re-introduction programme.

Under the copper-coloured beeches of the Upper Derwent Valley, the seeds known as beechmast produced by this most handsome of trees are a ready source of food

Red squirrels, currently considered extinct in the Peak District, could make a return in the future

Right: Beech trees add a splash of extra colour to the Upper Derwent Valley in autumn

Below: Great tits form large flocks with other members of their family during autumn and winter

for many birds. Great, blue and coal tits join large flocks of chaffinches and in some years, small numbers of brambling. These attractive birds breed in Scandinavia, where they are a common species, but during severe winters or when their local food crops fail, they migrate south to Britain and central Europe. They usually occur in mixed flocks with chaffinches but can be distinguished by their white rumps and speckled brown head which turns black at the onset of spring.

As autumn progresses, the beechmast becomes more difficult to locate among the fallen leaves. The tits have to forage deeper into the leaf litter, turning the leaves and searching out the remaining seeds. Once a seed has been found the tit returns to the relative safety of a nearby tree where it grips the seed with its foot and then proceeds to crack it open with its bill to extract the kernel inside. By contrast, the finches remain on the ground, using their more powerful beaks to prise open the seeds.

Although uncommon in the Peak, the most impressive member of the finch family is the elusive hawfinch. Secretive by nature, the hawfinch always presents a challenge to locate, but arguably the best time to look for them is during the autumn when they are most likely to be encountered feeding on the ground. The hawfinch is a large bird, equipped with a massive metallic-looking bill which is capable of cracking open cherry stones. They feed on an assortment of autumnal seeds and fruits, including haws, from which they derive their name, and they are also particularly fond of hornbeam.

Although the Peak District is well renowned for its nationally-important breeding populations of several species of wading birds, such as golden plover, the shortage of suitable wetland habitat makes the region less attractive to passage birds. One exception is Middleton Moor near Stoney Middleton, now owned by Glebe Mines. Although originally thought to be disastrous for wildlife, the mineral extraction has in fact benefited birdlife in the long term. The waste products that resulted from the extraction and washing of minerals settled into mud flats, forming two tailing lagoons which attract wading birds, gulls and wintering wildfowl.

In 1992, Laporte Minerals (the original owners) donated money to the Bakewell Bird Study Group to build a hide on the edge of No.3 lagoon from where many of the breeding birds including tree pipit, skylark, wheatear, whinchat and lapwing can now be seen. Later in 1994, with financial assistance from the Derbyshire Ornithological Society, a second hide was built overlooking No.4 lagoon. Each year in September an all-day bird watch takes place from this hide in an attempt to record as many bird species as possible. 1996 was a record year with 43 species seen including ten different waders, flocks of finches, raven and large numbers of gulls coming in to roost at dusk.

A male hawfinch gives a rare glimpse of his colourful plumage and powerful bill

Post-breeding flocks of lapwings can be seen at Middleton Moor

Rare Species and Re-introductions

U nfortunately in the recent past, a small number of endangered species have been lost from the Park, including dormouse, red squirrel and black grouse. The dormouse is now the focus of a re-introduction project in the Staffordshire part of the Peak District and forms part of the National Dormouse Recovery Programme. This project is being run by the People's Trust for Endangered Species and Royal Holloway University of London with the support of English Nature's Species Recovery Programme and the National Trust.

A total of 37 captive-bred dormice were brought to a site, identified as containing suitable habitat with good stands of hazel, in July, 2002. They remained in cages for 10 days to acclimatise, during which time they were fed an appetising daily mix of peanuts, sunflower seed, rich tea biscuits, apples and grapes. When their 10 days were up, holes were made in the release cages to allow them to come and go as they pleased. Food was then made available while they got used to their woodland territories and found new wild food supplies.

Over 200 boxes have now been put up around the site to provide nesting sites and to allow monitoring of the dormice. Each released dormouse has been given a unique identity chip so they can be recognised in future checks on boxes. Initial monitoring in autumn 2002 re-located some of the released mice as well as others that were the young of successful litters. Continued checks over the coming years will hopefully provide us with the good news that dormice are prospering in their new home.

Unlike the dormouse, the demise of the red squirrel was primarily as a consequence of the introduction and spread of a rival species, the grey squirrel. Any re-introduction programme would therefore have to take this into account. Simply releasing red squirrels into areas frequented by greys would almost certainly be unsuccessful. Only by effectively eradicating grey squirrels and maintaining their absence from a given location would it be feasible to consider re-introducing the red squirrel back into the Peak.

The situation concerning black grouse is less straightforward. The fortunes of this charismatic species have been documented for many years. There were two or three leks (display areas) present in the Park in the 1970s, but by the late 1980's this was down to a single site at Big Fernyford in the Staffordshire Moorlands, thus isolating the population. The lack of new blood led to in-breeding and lower productivity as a result.

During the early 1990s, although there were still up to ten males displaying at the lek, there were only two or three females. This population reduced through the 1990s and by the end of the millennium, black grouse were considered extinct in the Peak District.

Although moves are afoot to facilitate a possible re-introduction a number of key issues must first be addressed. Firstly, what exactly were the factors that contributed to the grouse's demise and can these be countered? Secondly, appropriate sites need to be identified and restored to allow a sustainable grouse population to exist across the Peak District. This could be achieved through a combination of sensitive management and co-operation from landowners, farmers and gamekeepers backed up by financial support from DEFRA.

This early part of the twenty-first century is crucial for many such species on the brink but we do have an opportunity, maybe our last, to do something positive to help these endangered species and perhaps redress some of the wrongs of the last century.

Above: *Will black grouse be seen again displaying in the Peak District?*

Opposite page: *Hazel dormice are doing well following their recent re-introduction*

Above: *Passage waders such as redshank were once regular visitors to the lagoons which have sadly become overgrown in recent years*

Above right: *Young hedgehogs have a race against time to put on the extra fat to help them through the winter*

Over the past few years the lagoons have become overgrown, which has unfortunately made them less attractive to wading birds. Despite this, it is still possible to see flocks of over 100 golden plover as well as good numbers of curlew, redshank, lapwing and snipe. From late autumn and throughout the winter, brightly-coloured shelduck frequent the pools alongside mallard, teal and small numbers of wigeon. Lesser black-backed and black-headed gulls still use the lagoons as an overnight roost, but their numbers, like the waders, have fallen in recent times as Carsington Water to the south of the Peak District has taken over as the place to roost.

During the autumn, hedgehogs begin preparing for hibernation by laying down sufficient fat reserves to see them through the winter. It is at this time of the year that they may be seen visiting gardens with increased regularity as they seek out a plentiful supply of food. They find their food by haphazard searching, relying on scent and sound to detect prey. Earthworms are a favourite along with slugs and snails, although small birds and mammals are also taken. Although they are chiefly meat eaters, fruit, berries and nuts also form part of their diet during autumn which helps them put on extra weight.

The hedgehog's instinctive defence mechanism is to roll up into a tight ball, a strategy which discourages all but the most tenacious of predators from attack. The sharp spines which form this defensive barrier are actually modified hairs that cover the upper parts of the animal except its head, which it can protect when necessary by tucking under its body.

With the exception of humans and more specifically our motorised vehicles, hedgehogs face very few threats, although occasionally one may fall prey to a fox or badger.

A hedgehog skin that has been neatly turned inside out and eaten clean is the work of a hungry badger. Indeed, hedgehog meat is said to be very good and provided a hearty meal for gypsies who baked them wrapped in mud over an open fire.

Most hedgehogs are born during mid-summer but some may be born much later and these are often the individuals that can be seen foraging for food during daylight hours. It is a race against time for these late arrivals, because they must reach a minimum weight of 450g to be able to sustain the long winter hibernation. By November most hedgehogs will be ready for their winter slumber, although mild spells of weather may see them linger a few weeks longer. They build a secure nest in a well-protected site such as a hedge bottom, compost heap or under a garden shed, which they line with dry leaves. Once this is completed, they tuck themselves into a ball, lower their heart rate and begin the long sleep through to spring.

As September slides into October there is often a noticeable drop in temperature which coincides with the rapidly decreasing daylight hours. The first frosts of autumn kill off many of the adult insects that provided the bounty of food for the summer migrants. Changes are taking place throughout the countryside and this is most evident in the rapidly changing colours of the Park's woodlands. The millions of fresh green leaves which emerged so quickly in spring and matured to cloak the deciduous trees in summer are now slowly dying as the trees cease production and enter their own state of hibernation.

The striking red hips of dog rose are covered in the first frost of autumn

Before the leaves are ripped unceremoniously from the branches by autumn gales, their ever-changing colours delight us with a display of yellows, russets and deep reds. This often-rapid change is brought about by a chemical reshuffling taking place within the leaf, a process triggered by day length. Temperature and rainfall also play a role in this triggering process as well as affecting the intensity of the colours, but it is the ever-shortening number of daylight hours that initiates the subtle train of events.

In response to the shorter daylight, the green chlorophyll that gives the leaf its green colour for much of the spring and summer gradually breaks down and is not replaced. As a result the green fades away leaving other more stable pigments behind. The yellow, orange and red colours which now come to the fore have been present all summer performing functions of their own, but they were masked by the abundant green chlorophyll. Now for a few weeks at least, they have the chance to glow and dazzle as the sun shines through the thinning canopy. The woodlands become a rich palette of colour as each tree develops its own unique colour scheme.

A thin veil of mist hangs over Padley Woods at dawn

The oak and beech woods of Padley Gorge are a riot of colour through late October and into November; the fading leaves falling to form mosaics of orange and brown on the wet rocks of Burbage Brook. On the moorland fringes silver birches shimmer in the breeze their vibrant yellow leaves dancing against a deep blue sky. Rowan leaves develop a deep red hue for a brief time while in the coniferous plantations of the Upper Derwent, the deciduous larches turn yellow and then a bright orange, contrasting perfectly with the evergreen foliage of the regimented lines of Sitka spruce.

Before the leaves finally drop to the ground, they perform one further vital role by serving as a mobile waste disposal system, ridding the tree of many toxic waste by-products such as tannins. These chemicals were important components of the leaves earlier in the year but now are no longer required and need to be disposed of. As the leaves are carried away on autumnal breezes the trees are left bare, a mere skeleton of their past glories, while underneath the woodland floor is littered with millions of decomposing leaves.

The woodland floor is carpeted with oak and beech leaves returning vital nutrients to the soil

Above: *The larch is the only conifer to shed its needle-like leaves in autumn*

Left: *Padley Woods fall quiet in autumn after the exuberance of summer*

Managing the Moors

Traditionally, moorlands have been managed to maximise red grouse numbers, and many of the techniques employed still have a key role to play in maintaining a healthy moor.

For example, the controlled burning of strips of heather in late winter removes old woody growth and creates a patch-work of heather of different ages. This produces young shoots for red grouse to feed on in spring while leaving longer heather for nesting. In contrast, areas of heather moorland which do not receive cyclic burning can quickly deteriorate in quality, leading to a reduction in grouse as well as other wildlife.

Sheep have grazed the moors for thousands of years, but their numbers have gradually increased with large numbers of ewes now grazing the moorland throughout the winter. This overgrazing removes vegetation, exposing the peat and leading to erosion. Accidental fires, such as the ones that raged across Bleaklow and other parts of the Dark Peak during Easter 2003, pose a more sinister threat, killing off plants and seeds and burning deep into the peat causing further erosion.

Visitors too can have a detrimental effect on the upland landscape. Thousands of pairs of feet walk the moorland footpaths each year. The scars left behind through trampling are clear to see along popular routes, as people trying to avoid becoming engulfed in mud create ever-widening paths. Erosion of this kind has serious implications for wildlife as well as landowners

and farmers as the loss of vegetation means there is less food for sheep and grouse and so fewer can live on the moor.

In 1987, the Moorland Management Project was set up to encourage good management and ensure the long-term survival of our moorlands. In some areas, English Nature in partnership with other organisations has initiated several moorland restoration projects in an attempt to address some of the most serious problems. These projects focus on a number of SSSIs in the Dark Peak and Eastern Peak District moors which have been damaged by overgrazing, accidental fires and access.

The simplest project on Kinder Scout involved limiting sheep numbers – an astonishing total of 38,000 sheep were removed from the hill by the Trust. This resulted in an increase in the cover of wavy hair-grass, heather and bilberry and an increase in red grouse numbers. Trials

elsewhere have concluded that eroded areas of moorland can be revegetated by reducing or removing grazing pressure; mechanical spreading of heather and wavy hair-grass seed; and planting a nurse crop of grass to stabilise bare ground to which heather, bilberry and other moorland specialists are added later.

There are approximately 12,000 ha of deep peat habitat throughout the Dark Peak, of which over 4100ha will be covered by these restoration projects. Through the establishment of the North Peak Environmentally Sensitive Area (ESA) in 1988, and another ESA in the South West Peak in 1992, DEFRA provides financial support to farmers who implement land management that conserves and restores moorland habitat.

The reduction of sheep stocking levels as well as the exclusion of grazing from selected areas is also a main feature of these ESAs. It is to be hoped that measures such as these will help to restore vital habitat for the specialised plants and other wildlife which manage to exist in the often hostile environment of the Peak District moorlands.

Above: *Pressure from over-grazing by sheep often leads to long-term moorland degradation*

Opposite page: *Controlled burning of old heather encourages new growth for red grouse to feed upon in spring*

Over the coming months, these will be slowly broken down by fungi thereby returning valuable nutrients to the soil and to the roots of the trees from which they have fallen. Throughout the autumn the strange fruiting bodies of fungi can be seen sprouting from damp bark and rotting trees stumps across the woodland floor. Unlike true plants, fungi have no chlorophyll and are unable to photosynthesise to produce energy and so must absorb nutrients from other lifeforms.

Their mycelia threads spread through the soil digesting organic matter and performing the role of natural re-cyclers of the essential components of life. Without them the countryside would be overwhelmed with dead material and it is only now in autumn that we are reminded of their importance as the bizarre and often colourful 'toadstools' emerge from the unseen mycelia to cast their spores into the damp woodland air.

Backlit against the golden glow of autumn foliage, a stag's steamy breath explodes into the cool dawn air as his mighty bellow echoes around the woodland. Complete with a thick dark mane and with his antlers at their most impressive, the red deer stag is a handsome animal, well deserving of the title, 'Monarch of the Glen'. There may not be any glens in the Peak District but there are certainly red deer and the best locations to watch them in action are Chatsworth and Lyme Parks. A visit to

Above: *The fruiting body of fly agaric contains highly poisonous toxins*

Right: *During October red deer are in the midst of their annual rut, a time when the highly-charged stags secure their mating rights*

one of these attractive parks in autumn may well be rewarded with some exciting encounters with Britain's largest land mammal.

October heralds the start of the rutting season for red deer and this is the time when the stags are most active as they noisily proclaim their presence and defend their territories from rivals. From late spring onwards the stags grow a fresh set of antlers that reach full size by the end of July. During August, the velvet covering which protects the developing antlers is shed, providing a meal for scavenging jackdaws. By October the stags are fully equipped for combat and the rut can begin in earnest.

During the rut, the stag's neck and mane thickens and his larynx develops to serve him with an impressively-deep roar. Although mainly silent at other times of the year, the stag roars incessantly during the rutting season as he attempts to impress the hinds (females). Periodically, the stag indulges in bouts of wallowing in peaty pools that make him appear black and fearsome. Each stag has a favourite wallow where he will roll from side to side, covering his coat with thick mud.

A bellowing red deer stag

Stags and hinds are only usually seen together during the autumn, spending the rest of year segregated in their own territories. As the rut approaches, the stags move into the hind's territory, each mature male occupying and defending a given area. His territory is clearly marked by roaring and by spraying urine and scent marking from a gland in his back feet. The stag also deposits scent on trees by thrashing his antlers against the lower branches.

Although each stag's territory is clearly defined, young pretenders often try their luck and challenge a dominant stag to a duel. These rutting rituals are usually no more than a show of strength as the dominant stay quickly demonstrates his superior strength while the challenger retreats to nurse his pride. Occasionally, when two stags are evenly matched these duels may continue for some time with each animal inflicting severe blows to its rival's flanks.

The triumphant stags then round up as many hinds as they can manage, which can be up to fifty, but is more typically around twenty. This is an arduous period for the stags as they continually patrol their territory, bellowing and preventing any of the younger stags from mating with 'their' hinds. By the time the rutting season draws to a close, the dominant stags are exhausted and will have lost condition and a great deal of weight. The pregnant hinds subsequently begin an eight-month gestation period before giving birth to a single calf in the following summer.

Chatsworth Park is home to a large herd of red deer

The park deer of Chatsworth and Lyme are largely a relic from medieval times when the King and other noblemen reserved much of the Peak District as the Royal Forest of the Peak for their exclusive hunting. Indeed, the origins of deer stalking date back to the reign of William the Conqueror. Vast areas were enclosed to form deer parks so that the privileged few could enjoy prime hunting. These days the herds at Chatsworth and Lyme have to be humanely managed to ensure a healthy population; the venison providing a useful resource for the estate.

The Chatsworth Estate is equally productive for birds of prey with several species breeding in the mixed habitats of woodland and moorland. However, one raptor which was a noticeable absentee until quite recently is the buzzard, a species that is widespread across western Britain but which had been very slow to colonise the Peak District. However, since the late 1990's, the number of breeding pairs has increased significantly and it is hoped that this trend will continue as young birds establish new territories.

On clear late winter days and throughout the spring, buzzards spend a good deal of their time engaged in territorial aerial activity above their chosen nest site, their

Buzzards are becoming a more regular sight over the western Peak District

Kestrels are the only British birds of prey which are able to hover for long periods

mournful mewing calls filling the air. After the spectacular aerial displays and noisy territorial disputes of spring, the summer months are relatively quiet as the pair settle down to raise their chicks. By early autumn however family parties can be seen on the wing close to their breeding site. At this stage the chicks are still unable to hunt successfully and they continue to beg for food, their piercing high-pitched calls reverberating over the wooded hillsides.

As autumn advances they begin to learn some of the necessary skills required to hunt and find food. During this critical period in their young lives many rely on searching for worms and beetles in fields before they hone their skills on larger prey. During the mellow days of autumn most adults will tolerate their young within their territory as long as there is sufficient food to support them. However, before the end of winter, the young buzzards are driven out by the male and are forced to search for a suitable territory of their own.

The gritstone edges of the Dark Peak are a favoured haunt of the Peak District's most widespread bird of prey, the kestrel. They are most noticeable during the autumn when several juveniles can be seen hovering close together. The strong updrafts along the likes of Derwent Edge and the Roaches provide the perfect conditions for young birds to master the art of hunting for small mammals.

By facing into the wind and using their fanned tail as a rudder these aerial supremos are able to hang effortlessly in a fixed position for several minutes. On spotting a movement below, they lower their position, hovering just a few metres above the ground. Starring intently into the grasses they wait for the right moment to strike. Then, without warning, they drop like a stone hitting the ground with out-stretched talons to clasp their prey. The young birds have a much lower strike rate compared to the more experienced adults but these are ideal places to practise. More crucially for the juveniles, they must have perfected their hunting skills by autumn's end if they are to survive the hardships of winter.

Kestrels prey predominately on small mammals, especially field voles that occur in large numbers in grassland habitat. These rodents, like their woodland cousins the bank vole and wood mouse, are far less active during the winter, instead relying on reserves of fat they have laid down during the plentiful autumn harvests. This makes life much tougher for kestrels and other predators and is the reason why some species such as the short-eared owl choose to vacate the moors in autumn, heading to the milder coast where there are easier pickings.

Weighing less than a two pence coin, the harvest mouse is one of the smallest rodents in the world. Their traditional home is the wheat fields of southern Britain but changes in the way that cereal crops are harvested has forced these delightful creatures to find refuge in field margins, hedgerows and wetland habitats. Recent searching during the winter for their summer-time nests has revealed their presence at two sites in the Derwent Valley and it is thought that they may well be present elsewhere.

For much of their lives they remain hidden in deep vegetation, making them almost impossible to spot. However, the presence of their tennis-ball shaped nests suspended from tall grass stalks provides confirmation of their existence. Using her prehensile tail and hind feet for support, the female shreds leaves into long strips which are left attached to the main stem and are then woven to form the framework to the nest. Working from the inside, she completes the domed nest, lining it with chewed vegetation, where she gives birth to her litter in late summer.

The autumn is also an important season for the region's bats, many of which are in the middle of their mating period. Male noctule bats, for example, establish a mating roost in a tree hole, which they defend from other mature males. Each evening soon after sunset, the male emits a series of shrill mating calls and produces a strong odour, attracting a harem of up to twenty females, which stay with him for one or two days. At the onset of winter most bats will have retired to the sanctuary of caves, tree holes and buildings where they will hibernate for four or five months, often at sub-zero temperatures.

Chapter 5

WINTER
The Big Sleep

For the human inhabitants of the Peak District, December is a colourful month of celebration, bright decorations and office parties: a time for over-indulging and relaxing in warm, cosy environments. For the wildlife which surrounds us, life could not be more different.

Cold damp weather, long dark nights and a less abundant supply of food brings hardship for many birds and animals. An ever-changing climate may have brought milder weather over the past decade, and with it, changing fortunes for some species. But the winter remains the toughest season for the wildlife of the Peak District, and it must adapt if it is to survive to the spring.

Left: *Severe winter weather forces many birds to flee the Peak District*

Opposite page: *The Wheel Stones form an imposing feature on the Derwent Moors*

The robins which visit the garden in winter may well have travelled from further north

Some mammals, such as badgers, retreat deep inside their underground chambers during periods of extremely cold weather, only venturing outside when the weather improves or when they are forced to search for food. Others, including the water vole, store vast quantities of food inside their riverbank home, which it can feed on periodically throughout the winter.

A more extreme means of dealing with the cold and lack of food is to shut down altogether and hibernate. Hedgehogs and dormice are classic examples of mammals which lay down substantial fat reserves during the autumn and then retire to a warm protected nest where they reduce their metabolism to a minimum level, thereby conserving vital energy.

Survival strategies such as these are extremely effective means of coping with the problem, but for birds these are not an option and they must employ other survival mechanisms. Long before the onset of winter many birds migrate to southern locales where there is a ready supply of food. This in itself is a very dangerous strategy, particularly for long distance migrants such as the swallow. Although birds are superb navigators, they rely on the sun and the stars to guide them to their destination. Strong winds blow them off course while rain, fog and thick cloud forces them down into unknown territory and potential hazards.

Moorland waders have less arduous journeys, departing to the coast or lowland wetlands where they feed on the rich pickings on the tidal mudflats, reservoir edges and damp meadows. Many predators must also leave to follow their main prey. Merlins and peregrines are regularly seen at the coast during the winter hunting pipits, larks and wading birds. Short-eared owls also find it impossible to survive on the moorlands in winter, when their chief prey, the field vole, is tucked away out of sight for long periods.

Even some of the birds which are considered to be residents migrate short distances. The robin which is seen in the garden during the summer may not be the same as the one that feeds from the bird table in winter. Many small bird species that breed here migrate south into continental Europe after the breeding season, while birds that spend the winter with us may well have crossed the North Sea from Scandinavia. Those that do choose to remain locally will however have a head start in spring, establishing territories and locating the best nest sites before the southern 'softies' return.

The winter mantle in Edale is a far cry from the welcoming meadows and pastures of summer

Face-to-face with... Tawny Owls

The 'tu-whit-tu-woo' call of the tawny owl is a sound that is familiar to everyone, often stemming back to childhood stories. Parents up and down the country imitate this call to their young children when bringing to life tales of the wise old owl of the woods. These early memories remain with us throughout our lives, leading in part to the universal popularity of these charismatic birds.

A couple of years ago, I had the chance to photograph a pair of tawny owls at their nest site in the Woodlands Valley of the northern Peak District. A chance meeting with a local gamekeeper led me to a nest containing two young owlets which he had discovered earlier that day. The nest was in a rotten birch stump only four feet off the ground and looked like the perfect site for photography.

So, over the course of the following week a colleague and I erected a small platform hide which provided us with a clear view of the chicks in the nest. The hide was then left in place for several days to allow the owls time to become accustomed to it.

Photographing nocturnal species presents a number of problems, not least the lighting. For this project, I used two flashguns mounted on poles that were attached to the frame of the hide. I also set up a red light to allow me to see the owls as they alighted as well as enabling me to focus the lens.

Setting up all this equipment on each visit was a tiresome task which had to be completed quickly and well before nightfall. Once the flash and camera were in position, I settled down to await the arrival of the adults.

I didn't have long to wait as within half an hour one of the parents returned with prey, which it dropped into the nest for the chicks. At this stage the chicks were able to feed themselves, and the adult quickly departed before I could obtain more than a single shot. On the following three visits, the adult landed with its back to the camera, preventing me from taking any further pictures that night. A subsequent session in the hide proved equally frustrating, with only a handful of pictures obtained. Fortunately, my third visit proved to be more successful. Shortly after dark, an adult swooped in through the trees and landed perfectly on top of the tree stump, giving me time to obtain my best shots.

A week or so later I returned to find the nest empty, the chicks having gained enough strength to clamber from the hollow stump into nearby trees from where they would continue to be fed by their parents. Tawny owlets regularly leave the nest before they can fly and unfortunately some fall to the ground where they may succumb to predators. This is certainly a hazardous time for young tawnies, but once they have developed a full set of flight feathers they are fully-equipped to begin to explore their woodland world.

An adult tawny owl perched above its two chicks as they clamour to be fed

To help them cope with the cold, birds feathers have excellent insulating properties, as is demonstrated by traditional eiderdowns. Many birds, especially smaller species, also produce more feathers in the winter and some may almost double the weight of their plumage in an effort to stay warm. Furthermore, by fluffing up their plumage, air is trapped between the feathers, adding further insulation. Some species keep warm by huddling together on sub-zero nights. Long-tailed tits and treecreepers often adopt this method, but the record goes to the wren. In the winter of 1969, a total of 96 wrens were recorded roosting together in the loft of a house, and others were still queuing up to get in!

During cold weather, small birds such as robin, dunnock, wren, tits and finches have to feed frantically as dusk approaches so that they have sufficient fat reserves to see them through the long night. By dawn these small birds will have used up their energy reserves and must immediately find food.

In fact, on cold winter days they feed almost continuously, consuming many times more food in an equivalent time than on a warm spring day. The bird table can sometimes become a battle ground as rival birds squabble for dominance on the

Above: *Many species benefit from the provision of peanuts and other foods*

Right: *Life in winter is tough for small birds like this greenfinch*

As dusk approaches thousands of starlings flock together before heading of to find warmth in our towns and cities

Foxes are regular visitors to many urban and suburban gardens, although they have a harder time breaking into the modern plastic dustbins

Above: *A male stonechat fronts it out while its relative, the whinchat opts for warmer climes further south*

Right: *Waxwings are occasional winter visitors from eastern Europe*

feeders. This inevitably ensures that the strongest survive while the weak and sick succumb to the elements or predators.

Starlings have perhaps adopted the most sensible strategy for keeping warm in winter by roosting in our towns and cities, where the temperature is always much warmer than the surrounding countryside. Huge flocks congregate each evening, wheeling in unison against the reddening sky, before they fly off to roost high on the buildings of Sheffield city centre. Pied wagtails have also taken to roosting in large numbers in urban areas, and have even learnt to exploit heated greenhouses and factories.

Our towns and villages become important refuges for other wildlife species during the winter. Foxes, once the denizens of the countryside, are now frequently seen scavenging food from dustbins and picking over discarded chip wrappers. Some move in just for the winter while others take up residence and may raise a family under a garden shed. Badgers too, are becoming more regular visitors to suburban gardens and many now come to feed on a mixed diet of jam sandwiches and peanuts offered by people keen to watch these fascinating nocturnal creatures.

Birds are also attracted to our gardens in winter but not just the regular species. In periods of extreme cold weather, fieldfares and redwings desert the countryside in favour of the berry-clad ornamental cotoneaster and pyracantha bushes. They may be joined in some winters by the elegant waxwing, an irregular visitor form Russia. In times of food shortage in their native country, waxwings migrate to Britain by the thousand and many descend on the Peak District, invariably turning up in urban areas where there is an abundance of berries. They often perch in tall trees, waiting for the opportunity to swoop down and quickly devour 15-20 berries at a time before retiring to digest their meal.

Sub-zero temperatures and bitter easterly winds force all but the hardiest of birds to flee the moorlands, which are left largely devoid of life during mid-winter save for the resonating calls of red grouse. Ravens too maintain their presence on the higher moors of the Dark Peak and a few meadow pipits can also be found lurking among the heather. Small numbers of stonechats spend the winter ekeing out a meagre existence along some of the gritstone edges. These dumpy birds which breed in low numbers in the Peak District have a robin-like shape and the male sports a distinctive black hood.

Above: *Red grouse footprints betray the presence of these hardy game birds on the high plateau of Kinder Scout*

Left: *The feathered legs of red grouse help keep them warm during winter*

Face-to-face with... Birds in the Garden

As the weather turns colder and wild foods become more difficult to find, many birds begin to visit bird tables to supplement their natural diet. Peanuts, sunflower seeds, suet, cheese, breadcrumbs and windfall fruits are just some of the ingredients which can be supplied.

These will readily be taken by tits, finches, thrushes, nuthatch, great spotted woodpecker, jay, dunnock, starling, robin and wren. A regular and varied feeding regime is one of the best ways of observing these familiar species at close range, and is also an ideal way to photograph them.

For many years, I have made use of an overgrown allotment for photography. I began putting out peanuts and black sunflower seeds in the early 1990s and quickly attracted common species such as blue and great tit, greenfinch, dunnock and robin. It was while photographing these species that I was amazed to see bullfinches feeding on seeds which I had scattered on the ground. At first there was just a single pair, but before long, two or three pairs were coming to feed and they remained close-by for much of the day.

Previous to this, I had not heard of bullfinches feeding on black sunflower seeds, and to my knowledge, they had not been photographed visiting bird tables. During the course of my first winter, bullfinches were regular visitors, taking centre stage on the bird table and aggressively chasing off other would-be diners. Every few seconds another bird would try to land, only to be forced to retreat as the dominant bullfinch flew at it with open beak. Occasionally two bullfinches would lock bills and flutter spectacularly above the bird table in aerial combat.

I continued to set-up a feeding station at the allotment each winter and each year the numbers of visiting bullfinches continued to increase. The record count seen at any one time was nine pairs; some on the bird table, others perched nearby in the privet hedge. In all likelihood the number of individuals actually visiting the bird table was probably much higher and may have been as many as fifteen to twenty pairs – a heartening statistic for a species that is in national decline.

One other observation I made during this project was the ability of bullfinches and some other birds to hone in on the food so quickly. It got to the stage that at the start of each winter I could guarantee that bullfinches would locate the food within only a few hours of the sunflower seeds appearing on the bird table (for the first time in six months). How do they do that?

Once the feeding had been going for a couple of weeks the speed at which the birds arrived was even quicker. On my arrival at the allotment the bird table was always empty, but within less than a minute of putting the seeds out, several bullfinches flew in from the surrounding allotments to feed. I can only assume that they saw me coming and recognised that their next meal was literally just around the corner.

The bullfinch remains one of my favourite birds

Hen harriers frequent the Eastern Moors in winter, quartering the rough grass-lands for meadow pipits

Kestrels continue to hawk over the moors and they are joined by the hen harrier, a scarce winter visitor to the Eastern Moors. With only one confirmed breeding success in the Peak District over the past forty years, hen harriers remain a noticeable absentee during the spring and summer. Still heavily persecuted throughout much of its range, their population in England is kept artificially low by those who uphold rigorous predator control measures on the moors. But in winter, these much-maligned birds are able to freely quarter the rough grasslands of the Eastern Moors on aerodynamic wings in search of meadow pipits, field voles and other small prey.

The male harrier sports a ghostly pale grey plumage with long wings tipped with black. In stark contrast, the female has an altogether plainer brown appearance with a long tail and distinctive white rump that leads to the alternative name of 'ringtail'. In common with all birds of prey, the female is significantly larger than the male, an evolutionary modification that allows the pair to hunt for different prey. As dusk closes in, several harriers may sometimes be seen returning to their favoured roost site, before settling down to spend the long night in a sheltered tree.

High on the moors of Kinder Scout, mountain hares are emerging from their daytime hide-outs deep among the heather or from beneath the sanctuary of the gritstone rocks. Introduced into the Peak District in the late 1800s from its native Scotland, the mountain hare has colonised most areas of the high northern plateau.

Above: *Mild winters make the white-coated mountain hare highly conspicuous on the dark heather moors*

Right: *A pair of mountain hares shelter in a snow-covered grough*

The original reason behind their introduction was to provide further sporting interests for the growing numbers of marksmen of the Victorian era. Today, they are largely untroubled by the guns and on their favoured heather-clad uplands they have been able to thrive.

During the summer the mountain hare's coat is a greyish brown similar in appearance to the brown hare although the smaller size and shorter ears of the former easily distinguish the two species. Unlike the brown hare, the coat of the mountain hare changes with the seasons, adopting a bluish grey in autumn and assuming the almost pure white, save for the black ear tips, of the full winter pelage. This adaptation is shared with other mountain dwellers which rely on camouflage to remain undetected by predators. Mountain hares are highly prized prey for golden eagles, wildcats and foxes in the Scottish Highlands, so it pays to be well concealed.

The moors of the Peak District are a far safer habitat with few foxes and certainly no eagles or wildcats to worry about. Indeed, the need for camouflage is really unnecessary and it is surprising that the hares bother to turn white at all. The fact is they have little choice in this biological transformation. Hares do not have the luxury of deciding which coat to 'wear' on any given day but instead respond to the natural changes taking place around them. As the number of daylight hours decrease, the brown coat fades to grey and then gradually whitens and thickens to form its warm winter coat by December.

With a reduced number of predators, the main threat to the isolated Peak District population is posed by severe weather. Extended periods of snow cover and bitter easterly winds on the exposed Kinder Plateau can take its toll and lead to starvation while wet springs can lead to high mortality among the leverets. Many hares are also killed on the high roads that dissect their territories, particularly the trans-Pennine Snake Pass.

The snow-covered uplands of winter makes tracking hares much easier; their characteristic footprints which criss-cross the hillsides betray their whereabouts. Regular routes are easy to spot by the well-trodden hare 'footpaths' that link favoured feeding areas. These make the perfect locations to sit and wait especially early and late in the day when a hare may pass within a few metres, oblivious to your presence. By late March, the hares lose their winter mantle and they begin to engage in courtship. This activity reaches a peak during April and it is then that they are most easily observed, sometimes becoming surprisingly tame.

The number of hare footprints on the Kinder Plateau is clear evidence of a thriving population

The many reservoirs found in the Dark Peak act as mirrors on calm sunny winter days, reflecting the surrounding woods and hills perfectly in their cool peaty waters. Their primary function is of course, to provide water for the homes of the human population which surrounds the Peak District. Acidic in nature and consequently low in aquatic life, the Peak's reservoirs are not renowned for wildfowl, but in recent years there have been an increasing number of sightings of goldeneye, red-breasted merganser and goosander. All three species are blessed with striking plumage which is at its most impressive when illuminated by the low winter sun.

The Derwent and Longendale chain of reservoirs are among the best places to look out for these handsome winter ducks. Goldeneye are scarce winter visitors to the Peak District but are well worth seeking out. The male has a bottle green head and a distinctive white spot below his characteristic golden eye, while the head of the female is a deep brown. As they fly fast over the water, their wings make a loud musical whistle and their large white wing patches become very noticeable. On sunny winter mornings, the drakes perform a unique display to the females, throwing their heads back, calling loudly and splashing the water with their feet.

Ladybower Reservoir is the largest of the chain in the Upper Derwent Valley

Goldeneye are occasional visitors to the Dark Peak reservoirs

Ratty's Highland Retreat

The water vole was once a familiar sight on waterways throughout Britain, but over the last 30 years it has suffered a catastrophic decline. Recent surveys have revealed that there are far fewer water voles at many sites and that they have been lost from some historical locations altogether.

The reasons for these declines are complex, but certainly involve a combination of loss and fragmentation of bankside vegetation, altered river management and, most significantly, the spread of the alien American mink, an effective predator of water voles.

Fortunately, there are still parts of the Peak District where water voles appear to be doing relatively well. Good areas to look for them include the River Wye, Chee Dale and Lathkill Dale, along stretches of slow-moving water with lush bankside vegetation and an earthy bank where they can excavate their burrows. Here you may see the stocky, chestnut brown form of a water vole swimming purposefully along, or hear the characteristic sound of them plopping into the water.

A survey carried out by the Derbyshire Wildlife Trust confirmed that the decline of water voles in some areas was related to mink. The American mink was brought to the UK to stock fur farms in the 1950s but subsequently escaped and is now well-established throughout most of the country including the Peak District. Mink are good swimmers and the female is small enough to enter water voles' burrows where she predates both adults and young. A female with young of her own to feed can quickly decimate a water vole population, then move on to a new territory.

On a more positive note, the survey also revealed that a surprising number of upland streams were inhabited by water voles. Traditionally, water voles have been thought of as a lowland species, but this survey in the Peak District and work in Scotland has discovered that water voles can flourish at high altitudes if the habitat is right. Indeed, signs of water vole activity have been found along tiny moorland streams reaching as high as 600m above sea level on Bleaklow. It appears that these slow-flowing streams, fringed with rushes and grasses found in the Dark Peak and on the Eastern Moors, are ideal habitat for them.

Although seldom seen on these moorland streams, they leave a number of tell-tale signs. The most obvious clue is a pile of cylindrical-shaped droppings at well-used latrines along the banks. Although the upland population is difficult to confirm, the large size of some latrines suggest that favoured habitats hold good numbers of breeding females.

Following mink predation and habitat loss, many of the lowland populations have now disappeared leaving the upland populations isolated. Ultimately, this isolation may be their saving grace, as mink do not favour these exposed upland streams, making these habitats important last refuges for 'Ratty'.

Following the dramatic decline of water voles in many of their lowland habitats, it is encouraging to discover that they are faring much better on upland streams

The commercial conifer plantations which surround many reservoirs support good numbers of siskin

A coal tit prizes out the seeds from a pine cone

The male goosander closely resembles the goldeneye in the colour of its plumage, but the two species are unrelated and otherwise quite different. Goosanders belong to the family of mergansers which also includes red-breasted merganser and smew. Mergansers are fish-eating diving ducks equipped with long slender bills with serrated sides to aid catching and holding their slippery prey, an adaptation which leads to their collective name of sawbills.

During the winter, goosander numbers build up significantly and counts of up to twenty individuals have been recorded on Ladybower. Like goldeneye, goosander prefer to nest in holes in trees close to the water's edge and both species will also take readily to the provision of suitable nest boxes. Whereas goldeneye move north to breed in Scotland and northern Europe, small numbers of goosander remain in the Peak, where they breed along the Derwent and Wye.

The red-breasted merganser has bred in the Peak District since 1973, and can be seen on the Upper Derwent reservoirs from late March onwards. Both the female and male have large shaggy crests giving them a punk-rocker appearance. Although they don't breed until late May, male red-breasted mergansers perform a lively display well before the mating season. This includes convulsive movements of the head and neck, crest raising, bowing and bobbing, arching the wings and skating across the water creating a line of spray all to the accompaniment of loud purring calls.

The network of footpaths and cycleways which surround these reservoirs makes this an ideal location to explore the extensive coniferous plantations that are such a conspicuous feature of the Upper Derwent. Lower in wildlife value than their deciduous counterparts, conifer woodlands are nonetheless an important refuge for many birds. Large flocks of brightly-coloured siskin seek out pine seeds calling wheezily as they move among the branches. In years when there is a plentiful supply of conifer seeds, their close relative the crossbills can also be found, sometimes breeding in substantial numbers.

Irregular in their occurrence, crossbills may spend one or two seasons in an area if conditions are favourable, but will readily move on to find new seed-rich locations whenever necessary. Although closely related to finches, they have evolved a specially adapted bill in which the upper and lower mandibles cross over to allow them to open pine cones and extract the seeds. When in residence these brightly coloured parrot-like birds can be detected by their 'kip kip kip' calls from high in the trees.

Coal tits are the most common members of their family to be found in coniferous woodland and these, together with chaffinches, occur in good numbers throughout the Upper Derwent, where they often frequent the car parks looking for hand outs.

Much more secretive in nature is the mighty goshawk, a formidable predator of birds as well as rabbits and squirrels. The Peak District represents one of the most important locations in the country for breeding goshawks; a species that remains under continued pressure from egg collectors and illegal persecution. In the past, falconers also took many birds, a practice that has been illegal for some time but still continued until quite recently. Nowadays, DNA testing can be used to determine the origins of a particular bird and this has made the threat of prosecution a serious deterrent.

On clear February mornings, goshawks can sometimes be spotted circling high above their breeding territories in the Upper Derwent. They are much bigger than sparrowhawks and appear altogether stockier, with a barrel chest and broad wings. Hunting along the woodland edge and through forest clearings, goshawks fly at great speed and are capable of bringing down a pheasant as well as other birds of prey such as sparrowhawk and long-eared owl. In essence, they are very effective killing machines, and it is this ruthless trait that continues to bring them in to conflict with game shooting interests.

The early courtship displays of the goshawk are mirrored by a number of other bird species, some of which may be in the midst of their breeding season well before St Valentine's Day. For humans, 14 February is a day for chocolates, flowers or even a candlelit meal as we display our affections for our loved ones. For many of us this celebrated day and all that the advertising gurus can muster persuades us that we should make more of an effort and declare unrequited love to our nearest and dearest.

In the birding world, things are very different. Their displays are instinctive with the sole purpose of finding a mate with whom to produce offspring. For a few hardy individuals the depths of winter are the prime time for courting: passions are high and love is most definitely in the air. Resident bird species which establish their territories early in the year have a head start over many of the summer migrants, allowing them to raise two or even three broods. This is a definite advantage, but by nesting early these birds also run the risk of experiencing bad weather, which can seriously hamper their efforts.

Goshawks continue to be a target for egg thieves

Above: *A change to warmer weather has encouraged song thrushes to breed in mid-winter*

Above right: *The raven is once again a regular breeding bird after a long enforced absence*

The recent run of mild winters has facilitated some species such as blackbirds and song thrushes to nest in January and February. The warmer climate brings with it more food in the form of insects as well as more favourable weather conditions which will give the newly hatched chicks a far better chance of survival. These early nesters are obviously not making a conscious decision based on facts, but merely responding to the changes that are taking place in our climate.

This recent phenomena aside, there have always been birds that have chosen to nest early in the year simply because it suits them to do so. Most birds nest when there is maximum availability of food on which to feed their chicks. This is certainly true for crossbills which time their breeding season to coincide with the harvest of pine seeds in late winter.

Crossbills are not alone in their winter vigil for high on the exposed cliffs of the Dark Peak, hen ravens are also warming their eggs. As more material is added each year, the great fortress that makes up the raven's nest may be over five feet in depth. The blue-green eggs are bedded into a deep wool-lined cup on which the female sits tight, bracing herself against the worst of the late winter storms.

Ravens are birds of the open hill, reliant on the sheep industry of the uplands to provide them with rich pickings through the winter as animals perish through cold and starvation. By early spring, there is a second harvest of placentae and still-born lambs from the large flocks of hill sheep. This abundant carrion coincides with the arrival of the chicks which hatch out on exposed rocky cliffs. While the female broods her young, protecting them from the cold winds and rain, the male scavenges for food to bring back to the nest.

In contrast to the raven's winter solitude, the communally nesting rooks are calling vociferously and displaying with fanned tails throughout February, as they establish pairs and repair old nests scarred by winter gales. Despite their preference for nesting in colonies rooks, do not always make good neighbours for they are constantly squabbling and stealing twigs from each others nests. This aggressive behaviour subsides in March, by which time the females are quietly incubating their eggs.

Grey herons are also colonial nesters and a visit to one of the Peak's several heronries on a warm February day should be rewarded with plenty of activity. Arguably the best site within the Peak District is located at Trentabank Reservoir where a thriving colony has been in existence for well over 25 years. The reservoir, constructed in the 1930s as a source of water for the Macclesfield area, is surrounded by coniferous woodland. Once the trees reached sufficient height, the

A grey heron alights at its nest site

127

Natural versus Managed

Today, very few natural habitats exist which have been left untouched by the hand of Man. The question is, given the opportunity, should we allow natural order to restore wild places to their original state, or should we manage them to maintain particular habitats? In an ideal world it would be wonderful if we had the ability to turn back the clock and recreate wilderness areas. But in reality, this is simply not practical.

The best that we can do now is take steps to conserve what we already have and wherever possible, try to restore habitats, whether this is on nature reserves or in the wider environment. Like it or not, most land has to be actively managed in order to maintain or create a rich biodiversity of plants, insects, birds and animals. It is important, however, that we look at the whole picture and not simply at isolated nature reserves. If not, habitat fragmentation might result, where wildlife havens stand as islands in an otherwise featureless desert.

The key to successful wildlife conservation is habitat management. If specific habitats are managed sympathetically then the associated wildlife will flourish. Exactly how this is best achieved is open to debate. Buying a wonderful piece of habitat, putting a fence around it and leaving nature to take its course will not necessarily be the best way forward. Indeed, left to nature many habitats would eventually revert to woodland with certain species becoming dominant. This may be no bad thing, but will it benefit wildlife in general?

Over the centuries, human activities have inadvertently created a diversity of habitats which support a broad range of species. So if we want to maintain these partially 'artificial' habitats, then they have to be managed. However, conserving some species may well be to the detriment of others. In order to protect species-rich grasslands on nature reserves, for example, scrub must be removed. But left alone, dense thickets of hazel and hawthorn would dominate, attracting nesting birds, winter thrushes and providing shelter for mammals.

This is one of the many dilemmas facing reserve managers. The easy answer is to conserve both. If larger tracts of land were managed for wildlife then this may be an option. However, at the current time and with the limited resources available, difficult choices have to be made. Other searching

questions must also be answered. For example, should more effort be put into conserving rare species? Or would it be better to implement management techniques for a wider range of species?

To answer some of these questions a good deal of research and feasibility studies must take place before anything is decided. Sometimes it is a matter of trialing management techniques to find out what works and what doesn't.

With increased knowledge comes a better appreciation of how best to proceed but nature is a complex web of organisms and it takes time and experience to fully understand how a single management procedure may influence an individual species. We may think we have a good idea of what to do. But ultimately, does nature know best?

Above: *Left unmanaged, many areas would soon revert to woodland with the colonisation of silver birch, ash, hazel and hawthorn*

Opposite page: *Flower-rich unimproved grasslands such as the one pictured here on the DWT Priestcliffe Lees Nature Reserve have to be carefully managed to prevent the spread of scrub woodland.*

herons moved in and obviously found the situation to their liking with around twenty pairs now breeding each year.

The herons return each year towards the end of January and soon begin to repair or add to their old nests. Throughout February the herons remain active with nesting duties, as well as engaging in courtship display. At this time the bill of the male bird develops a deep red colour and the pair point their beaks towards the sky while fluffing out the feathers on their neck. This courtship display strengthens the bond between the pair and is often a prelude to mating and egg laying.

The Cheshire Wildlife Trust lease the site from United Utilities and manage the heronry as a nature reserve. Although there is no public access into the reserve (in order to prevent any undue disturbance), the birds can be viewed from the Heronry Viewpoint located a short distance along the Shutlingsloe footpath. Here the trees have been cleared to allow an eye-level view across to the nesting birds. By using binoculars or a telescope, bird watchers can gain an excellent insight into the daily lives of these fascinating birds.

Hazel catkins are a welcome source of pollen for insects and blue tits

The tawny owl is by the far the most vocal of the Peak District's five native owl species, its characteristic 'tu whit tu whoo' calls regularly breaking the silence of a winter woodland. This characteristic hooting begins in the autumn but reaches its peak during January and February when the pair engage in prolonged bouts of courtship, serenading each other with hooting followed by ke-wick calls. Deep within a hollow tree the female lays her clutch of two or three pure white eggs which she will incubate for around four weeks. During this time the male hunts for them both, bringing prey to the nest site for the female. For the time being he can hunt at leisure, but soon the hatching chicks will make his task more arduous as they demand a regular supply of food.

Underground in their cosy setts, newly-born badger cubs are making similar demands of their mother. Born blind and defenceless, badger cubs are wholly reliant on the sow for nourishment, suckling on her rich milk in the protective surroundings of the nursery chamber. On warm winter nights she will emerge to forage for food to help maintain this vital supply of nutrients for her growing cubs.

Periodically, she gathers new bedding by scraping together piles of dry grasses and bracken with her front paws, tucking the bundle under her chin and shuffling

A female badger collects fresh bedding for her young cubs

unceremoniously back down into the sett. Old soiled bedding that has been discarded near the sett entrance is a clear indication that there are cubs in residence, but it will be well into spring before they are seen above ground.

In stark contrast, snowdrops first appear in late January, their attractive white flowers emerging almost overnight in woodlands and gardens. Also known as Candlemas bells and February fairmaids, snowdrops are used to celebrate the Feast of Candlemas on the 2 February. They were probably first introduced into churchyards and gardens from southern Europe, where they are pollinated by insects. In our colder climate, they reproduce mainly by dividing their bulbs although their copious pollen attracts early flying insects on warmer winter days.

Other tentative signs that spring is just around the corner come in the form of a flush of yellow pussy willow and hazel catkins which decorate many hedgerows and woodland edges throughout February and March. These early flowering trees attract hardy insects to their colourful displays as well as birds such as blue, great and long-tailed tit. The latter form large roving flocks in winter, moving restlessly along the hedgerows picking off insects. As they feed they keep in contact with each other through a series of thin 'see see see' calls. In flight their long tails act as rudders to the fluffy ball of body feathers, taking them buoyantly between the trees.

Although the dawn chorus in a February woodland is less varied than later in spring, it can still be a surprisingly noisy time. Great spotted woodpeckers are the

By the end of January the specially hardened tips of snowdrops force their way through the frozen ground

chief protagonists as they engage in territorial drumming. By striking the tip of his powerful bill rapidly on a resonant branch, the male produces short bursts of staccato drumming and is capable of hammering out up to twenty blows per second. Great spotted woodpeckers are one of the few birds that have increased in population in recent years and are now common in almost all of our woodlands. They are also regular visitors to many gardens and use their stiff tails expertly as they cling to peanut feeders.

Joining the woodland chorus on warm winter mornings are the excited calls of grey squirrels as they indulge in their extravagant arboreal antics. The female takes the lead in their elaborate courtship rituals by goading her male suitors to chase her through the branches. As she cavorts across the treetops she leaves a perfumed trail that entices the males to follow in hot pursuit. She will lead them on a merry dance until finally she succumbs to the ardour of the fittest male. Following successful mating the female then becomes very assertive and she will drive out the male from her chosen nesting site which may be a specially constructed drey or an old woodpecker hole.

For many people one of their first experiences of the natural world is collecting frogspawn. Watching the incredible transformation from egg to tadpole and the

Above: *The resonating drumming of great spotted woodpeckers reverberates around the woodland in winter*

Left: *Grey squirrel passions run high during late winter as they engage in courtship*

133

Top: *The lack of ponds in the countryside has led to a reduction in frog numbers*

Above: *Dew ponds, once a common sight in the White Peak, are the focus of a restoration initiative*

subsequent metamorphosis into a frog was certainly one of the highlights of early biology lessons at school. Many children seem to develop a fascination for frogs and toads from these early encounters, although for others these slimy amphibians are creatures of nightmares, creating phobias that last into adulthood.

In reality there is nothing to be feared from the five amphibian species which inhabit the Peak District. In fact, they have far more to fear from us through habitat loss and from the vehicles that we drive. All amphibians require water in which to breed, but this is becoming an ever-declining commodity as ponds are filled in or neglected leading to a lack of suitable spawning grounds. This is compounded by the fact that thousands of frogs and toads are killed by traffic each spring as they attempt to cross busy roads on their return to traditional breeding ponds.

During 1998 staff at the Peak District National Park carried out a survey of ponds, taking a particular interest in dew ponds. These circular clay-lined ponds were originally created to provide drinking water for stock in limestone areas where there was little standing surface water. The survey discovered that half of the White Peak's dew ponds had disappeared over a 15-year period raising serious concerns for amphibian populations. The Park Authority is now undertaking a project to restore some of these dew ponds that have been identified as important breeding grounds for great crested and smooth newts as well as frogs.

A more positive change of fortune for some amphibians is the increase in the number of garden ponds. This has in some way compensated for the loss of ponds in the countryside, and has certainly greatly benefited the once-common frog. In early spring, these ponds are turned into boiling cauldrons of activity as male frogs croak and squabble. This usually takes place in late February with the males arriving first to strike up their 'love-songs' to attract the females. Once they have been wooed to the pond, the females are grabbed unceremoniously as the pair form a tight embrace, the male hanging on with specially developed 'nuptial pads' on each of his 'thumbs'.

The pair may remain in amplexus (paired) for several days until the female releases as many as 3000 eggs, which are fertilised by the male and form the characteristic clumps of jelly. Depending on the temperature of the water, the tadpoles emerge from the frogspawn two or three weeks later.

The migration and spawning of the common toad is an even more spectacular affair. Towards the end of March legions of these warty-skinned creatures leave their winter hideouts in walls, compost heaps or under logs and head for their communal breeding grounds. They may travel doggedly for several kilometres, usually on damp mild nights, until they reach their final destination, typically a large pond, reservoir or old mill pond with deep water.

While most males wait in the water for the arrival of the females, some adopt a cunning tactic, waiting in ambush along the route to hitch a ride on the larger female's back. This not only saves energy but also gives them the best chance of securing a mate. However, when the females arrive at the water they and their passengers are mobbed in what amounts to an almighty scrum. Larger males can dislodge smaller rivals from their mounts leaving the strongest, most tenacious individuals to fertilise the female's string of 800-2500 eggs.

The Peak District also supports all three of Britain's native species of newt: palmate, smooth and great crested. The great crested newt is afforded special protection and has the power to prevent development schemes and even divert roads which threaten its breeding pond. However, it is the palmate newt that is believed to be the least common, favouring the soft acidic waters found in many of the ponds in the millstone grit area. The male palmate newt is identified by a low smooth-edged crest down its back and webbed or 'palmate' hind feet.

By contrast, the male smooth newt has an undulating crest which runs from its head to the tip of its tail. It is also more colourful than the palmate newt with an orange belly, blue edged tail and is heavily spotted. The two also vary in water preference with the smooth newt most likely to be found in the alkaline ponds of the White Peak. At up to 15cm long, the great crested is the largest of our three newts. In the breeding season the male is particularly impressive, sporting a conspicuous jagged crest along his back and a bright orange belly dotted with black. Locally this species is found in the White Peak, preferring ponds that are not too acidic and free from predation by fish.

The courtship of all three newts is an elaborate affair, after which the female lays her eggs singly on aquatic plants, folding the leaf over them for protection from predators. Newt eggs develop into tadpoles in the same way as frogs and toads, and by late summer they will have metamorphosed into tiny newtlets or 'efts'. The young newts, like their parents, tend to remain close to their birthplace but it is two or three years before they are fully mature and ready to return to the water to participate in the annual affairs of our amorous amphibians.

Top: *Common toads may remain in amplexus for many hours or even days.*

Above: *Great crested newts often find refuge in dew ponds*

Chapter 6
CONCLUSION
Back to the Future

What does the future hold for the wildlife of the Peak District? This is the sixty four million dollar question and all anyone can do is predict what may happen based on current knowledge. Certainly we are better placed now to make accurate predictions than even twenty years ago. Research into individual species as well as ecosystems, habitats, climate and environmental issues has given us a much greater understanding of the natural world.

This knowledge and the support of a more environmentally-aware public could make a difference, but this alone may not be enough. Government policies must also become more environmentally-sensitive, and address key issues such as agriculture, transport and pollution.

The land that now forms the Peak District National Park has undergone major changes over the centuries, and it will continue to do so in the future. In modern history, people have shaped the landscape into what we see today, but some of the biggest changes have occurred as a result of a changing climate, and this may well be the case again in the future.

At the end of the last Ice Age, the Peak District was a barren landscape devoid of life but gradually over time the first plants, and animals began to colonise, forming distinct habitats with their own unique diversity of species.

This trend was continued by human activity developing a close relationship between the land, its wildlife and its people. New habitats were created at the expense of others and with these changes came a changing variety of plants and animals. Over the same period, peoples' attitude towards wildlife also changed. Originally seen as a source of food and raw materials, wildlife has been culled, persecuted, hunted, cut down, burnt and sprayed. Certain species have become extinct while others have flourished. Many have been introduced both intentionally and unintentionally, some with catastrophic consequences.

Above: *Much of the White Peak is a working landscape of small farms enclosed by dry stone walls*

Opposite page: *Another beautiful sunrise on the shivering face of Mam Tor. But what will the future hold for the Peak District?*

The return of peregrine falcons is one of many wildlife success stories of recent years

Twenty-first-century civilisation has also changed and as a nation we are more aware of the plight of the planet than ever before. But how may this more enlightened attitude affect the Peak District National Park in the future? One thing that has not changed in recent times is that the Park is a working environment, inhabited by people who need to make a living. It also attracts millions of visitors and will continue to do so. These are major land use issues that have a strong bearing on what may happen in the longer term.

How the land is used and managed will ultimately determine the future for the wildlife. Farming is still the biggest land use within the Peak District and as such has a major role to play. Other land uses such as limestone quarrying, lead mining, water supply, forestry and game shooting have created specialised habitats that support a rich diversity of wildlife. This diverse tapestry of habitats and wildlife is what makes the Peak District so special and it is this that we must act to protect and conserve.

Arguably the most significant land use change in recent times is the way in which the land is farmed, partly as a result of technological advances but more specifically because of government policies and EU directives. The use of herbicides and insecticides has altered the face of much of the farmed land and has led to the creation of a highly productive monoculture of rye grass that is of low value to wildlife. These changes have been at the expense of species-rich hay meadows and have led to serious declines in many farmland birds. Such losses are lamentable but unfortunately may well continue unless government food production policies change radically in the future.

Conservation organisations as well as some landowners and individuals are actively trying to halt these declines. Furthermore, projects such as the Hay Meadows Project (see page 62) and the Peak Birds Project (page 40) have gone a long way to highlight the problems and have begun to make a positive difference.

Other areas for concern including moorland degradation are also being addressed and funding has become available to aid the work of vital restoration projects. Key habitat conservation and restoration projects such as these form the cornerstone of long-term wildlife conservation and will hopefully reduce further losses in the future.

While the declining fortunes of some species continue to hit the headlines, it should not be forgotten that there have been a number of success stories in the Peak District in recent times. Perhaps the most significant has been the recovery of the region's birds of prey following their catastrophic collapse during the 1950s and '60s at the hands of organo-chlorine pesticides. The number of breeding pairs of peregrine falcons increased markedly during the1990s, with almost all of the suitable territories occupied. Merlins are also widespread on the upland moors although, like peregrines, they continue to be the target of illegal egg collectors.

Although goshawk numbers still remain low (as a result of egg thieves and persecution) their smaller relative, the sparrowhawk, is faring much better with a significant increase in population. It is now a regular sight over much of the Peak District as well as in suburban gardens.

An improvement in river quality and better river management has led to the comeback of the Peak's most elusive mammal, the otter

An even more remarkable recovery has been made by the buzzard, a species extermi-nated from the area by the end of the nineteenth century, but now making a welcome return. The number of breeding buzzards was restricted to only a handful of records up until the mid-1990s which saw the beginning of a rapid re-colonisation. By 2001 there were over twenty confirmed breeding pairs in the Peak District and this looks set to increase further over the coming years as birds move into new areas.

Ravens were also absent from the Peak for many years but returned to breed in 1994. There are currently around twenty pairs, mostly breeding on the high crag faces of Kinder and in some of the old quarries of the White Peak. Their resonating, honking calls can be heard throughout the winter and become most noticeable from late January onwards when pairs engage in spectacular aerial courtship displays.

Unfortunately, these rising fortunes are not shared by the hen harrier, a species which continues to suffer persecution throughout its range, making it difficult for it to make any sort of recovery. Although a few individuals overwinter on the Eastern Moors, none have bred successfully in the Peak District since 1997 when a much-celebrated pair raised four chicks in the Goyt Valley.

The fortunes of the region's mammals is somewhat mixed. Some, like the water vole, have suffered major declines but there are encouraging signs that the slow recovery of the otter from the south is beginning to gather momentum. Harvest mice have also been discovered breeding in the Park in small numbers and these will hopefully begin to increase and colonise other localities. The recent re-introduction of dormice into the Staffordshire part of the Peak is another success story, with small numbers now breeding.

Other re-introductions of species that have been lost from the Peak District may follow

The untamed Kinder Plateau is home to several pairs of ravens

in the future, most notably black grouse and red squirrel. These high profile species always attract a lot of attention, but any potential re-introduction programme must be approached cautiously to ensure a similar fate isn't suffered by individuals that are released into inappropriate habitat.

Other 'new' species may follow naturally. Indeed, the Peak District may not have to wait too long before the osprey is a regular breeder. A pair has bred in the Lake District for the last three years and if birds begin to breed regularly at Rutland Water in nearby Leicestershire, there may be young birds looking for new territories. Certainly, the well-stocked reservoirs in the Upper Derwent Valley as well as at Carsington Water just to the south of the National Park would provide an ideal habitat.

Will the pine marten return in the future?

Another Scottish speciality, the pine marten may also become a regular sight in some of the coniferous woodlands. Once widespread throughout Great Britain, pine martens were heavily persecuted during the Victorian era and only just managed to retain a foothold in north-west Scotland. A more relaxed approach to gamekeeping in recent times has seen their numbers increasing throughout Scotland, and they have now spread south into England with unconfirmed sightings reported from parts of the Peak District.

If the current trend towards warmer weather continues we may also witness other changes, both in the species present as well as populations and seasonal behaviour. Since the beginning of the 1990s, the Peak District has experienced much milder winters and this is certainly beneficial to some species such as mountain hare that live

A changing climate with warmer winters and more extremes of weather is likely to bring changes to the natural history of the Park

141

all year round on the exposed high plateaux. Common birds have also been affected in terms of the timing of their breeding season with some species now choosing to nest much earlier. Another recent phenomenon is the over-wintering of blackcaps and chiffchaffs, two species that would normally migrate to Africa.

Birds such as these feed mainly on insects (although blackcaps also feed on berries and fruit), and are the reason why many insectivorous birds migrate south. However, mild weather with fewer sub-zero nights means that more insects survive the winter and provide food for many birds and animals. As a result, we may begin to see more migratory birds spending the winter here. The downside of this warming climate is that more pest and disease species are also surviving, and this could cause problems for plants and animals in the future.

We may see similar increases in the populations of some plants which favour mild conditions. Conversely, some northern species such as cloudberry and alpine cinquefoil may be lost from the Peak. What is for sure is that we will inevitably see fluxes in the populations and ranges of some species as a consequence of both climatic and environmental changes in the future. This has certainly been the case for the past 10,000 years, as the fortunes of the region's wildlife have ebbed and flowed with the changes taking place around them.

The explosive seeds of Himalayan basalm are carried by water, germinating along river banks and crowding out native species

Another certainty is the continuing colonisation of so-called alien species. Historically, many non-native species were introduced deliberately into some parts of the country and subsequently expanded their range into the Peak District. Rabbit, grey squirrel, mink, signal crayfish, little owl, Canada goose and pheasant are just a few of the well-known species that have been introduced in the past. Some, like the little owl and pheasant, are welcome additions to the Peak's wildlife, while others such as mink and signal crayfish predate native species and are viewed as pests.

Many plants have also found their way into the wild, often from introductions into gardens. Rhododendron is one colourful and very evident species that causes major problems wherever it thrives, shutting out the light and limiting the growth of native plants. Annual rhododendron-pulling work parties are common on many nature reserves in an attempt to control this invasive species.

Himalayan balsam, a most attractive flowering plant brought to Britain in the eighteenth century, causes similar problems along riverbanks where it grows in profusion. Other contenders for the Peak's most loathed plants are Japanese knotweed, a highly-invasive species that is difficult to control, and giant hogweed, a Trifid-like plant of gargantuan proportions which shades out everything in its path.

The lives of people have always been inter-connected with the Peak District and not just for those that reside within the Park boundaries. The vast majority of people present on any given day are visitors, a great many from the surrounding cities of Manchester, Sheffield, Derby, Nottingham and Birmingham. A well-cited figure is that 22 million visits are made each year, of which 90 per cent are by car.

Tourism on this scale inevitably brings problems, not least through traffic congestion. Erosion of footpaths and sensitive vegetation can be considerable on well-trodden routes. Disturbance to wildlife, particularly nesting birds in spring, is also of concern particularly from loose dogs and activities such as a rock climbing, mountain biking and hang gliding.

While the majority of people are considerate visitors with a respect for the natural landscapes and wildlife, a minority can cause widespread damage. This has been starkly illustrated in past years with several large-scale and devastating moorland fires that have been attributable to discarded cigarette ends or have even been started deliberately. Fires such as these cause extensive damage to sensitive upland habitats that may take many years to recover.

Controversy over the Peak fires has been debated in the House of Lords, raising further questions of the impact of the new Countryside and Rights of Way Act, 2000. The majority of the Act concerns access to 'open' country: mountain, moorland, heath and down, with which the Peak District, of course, is well blessed. The Act will allow people the right to roam over open country, although landowners do have the sanction to restrict access for up to 28 days with permission from the National Park Authority.

Some suggest that the presently-restricted areas are refuges for wildlife, and that allowing open access will cause disturbance, further erosion and create an increased risk of fire. Others argue that there are already large tracts of the Peak with open access with plentiful wildlife, and that opening-up yet more areas can only serve to lessen the pressure by distributing visitors over a wider area.

It is clear that the Peak District remains as popular with visitors as ever before but what is needed is sustainable tourism. Recreation and tourism development must be

Lathkill Dale, like much of the Peak District attracts large numbers of visitors throughout the year

sympathetic to both the needs of visitors and the Park itself so that it is protected for future generations to enjoy. Sustainable tourism should ensure that the natural resources (habitats and wildlife) as well as the environmental, social and economic well-being of the Peak District are maintained forever.

Over the course of history, human activities have moulded the Peak District landscape, largely to suit our own needs and often with little regard for the welfare of wildlife. At the start of this new century we are able to take stock of the result of these activities on the wild places and wild creatures of this treasured National Park and look forward to the challenges ahead. We already have much to celebrate and as more people become aware of the rich natural heritage found within this English heartland, there will hopefully be much more to celebrate in the future.

A time to reflect